Jim Britt's

Cracking the Rich Code[13]

Inspiring Stories, Insights and Strategies from Top Thought Leaders Around the World

STAY IN TOUCH WITH JIM BRITT

www.JimBritt.com

www.JimBrittVentures.com

www.JimBrittCoaching.com

www.CrackingTheRichCode.com

www.PowerOfLettingGo.com

Cracking the Rich Code[13]

Jim Britt

All Rights Reserved

Copyright 2024

CTRC Publishing and Training, Inc.

10556 Combie Road, Suite 6205

Auburn, CA 95602

The use of any part of this publication, whether reproduced, stored in any retrieval system, or transmitted in any forms or by any means, electronic or otherwise, without the prior written consent of the publisher, is an infringement of copyright law.

Jim Britt

Cracking the Rich Code[13]

ISBN: 979-8-8693-7915-3

Co-authors from Around the World

Jim Britt

Deena Giordano Ullom

Carole Stizza

Helen Kagan

Gabriella Alziari

Ryan Lombardo

Steve Walsh

Cecelia "Fi" Mazanke

Dona L. Kappmeyer

Judy CopenBarger

Jim Carbaugh

Hylke Faber

Phillip Suggs

Rory Douglas

Jim Diebold

John Verrico

Angilie Kapoor

James Gray Robinson

Markiesha E Wilson

Mark Yuzuik

Merrilee of Solana

DEDICATION

Entrepreneurs will change the world. They always have and they always will.

Dedicated to the entrepreneurial spirit that lives within each of us. God Bless America and the World!

PREFACE

Jim Britt

The world's top 50 most influential speakers and top 20 life and success strategist.

In pursuit of a meaningful and fulfilling life, the concept of richness extends far beyond mere financial prosperity. It encompasses a holistic approach, embracing abundance in every facet of our existence—financial, emotional, intellectual, and spiritual. "Cracking the Rich Code with 21 Top Thought Leaders" is not just a manual for accumulating wealth; it is a comprehensive guide to attaining riches in all areas of life.

The journey to holistic riches is a transformative odyssey, and within these pages, you'll find the collective wisdom of 21 experts who have not only achieved remarkable success in their respective field but, have also cracked the code to living a truly rich and fulfilling life, while helping other to do the same. Their stories, insights, and strategies are the keys to unlocking doors to prosperity abundance and well-being.

Our esteemed contributors are visionaries who understand that true richness transcends financial accomplishments. Their perspectives span the spectrum, from business, to personal development, mindfulness, relationships, health and wellness, and spirituality. Each chapter in this book serves as a beacon of guidance, offering a unique perspective on how to navigate the intricate pathways of life to attain richness in all dimensions.

As you delve into the following pages, you'll be introduced to the stories of these remarkable individuals who have not only achieved success in their respective fields, but have also cultivated richness in their relationships, health, and sense of purpose. Their experiences are a testament to the idea that true wealth is a compellation of material prosperity and the riches found in our connections, personal growth, and the alignment of our actions with our deepest values.

True richness moves beyond the material realm into emotional richness. Emotional intelligence, resilience, and the ability to navigate the complexities of human relationships. Each coauthor offers practical tools and perspectives that will empower you to forge deeper connections, overcome challenges, and find joy in your everyday interactions.

Intellectual richness is also a dimension often overlooked in the pursuit of a rich life. From innovation and creativity to conscious learning and adaptability, intellectual richness is the fuel that propels us forward. All creation begins with an idea. The contributors share their insights into cultivating a curious mind, staying ahead of a rapidly changing world, and leveraging knowledge to create a life of richness and purpose.

Spiritual richness takes center stage too. Beyond religious affiliations, spiritual richness encompasses a profound connection with oneself, others, and the universe. These thought leaders share their journeys of self-discovery, mindfulness, and the pursuit of a higher purpose, offering a more rich and meaningful existence.

This book is not a one-size-fits-all prescription for richness; it a diverse tapestry of ideas, experiences, and strategies that you can tailor to your unique journey. Whether you are an entrepreneur seeking business and financial success, or an individual navigating the complexities of relationships. A lifelong learner, or someone on a spiritual quest, "Cracking the Rich Code" has something for you.

As you embark on this transformative journey with our diverse lineup of thought leaders and experts, just remember that richness is not a destination but a continuous exploration. May the insights and strategies within these pages serve as catalysts for your personal and collective growth, guiding you toward a life of richness in every sense of the word.

Wishing you abundance fulfillment, and richness in all areas of your life.

And remember, just one idea acted upon can change your life. Happy hunting!

Jim Britt

www.JimBritt.com

www.CrackingTheRichCode.com

www.PowerOfLettingGo.com

Foreword by Brian Tracy

Life is always a series of transitions... people, places and things that shape who we are as individuals. Often, you never know that the next catalyst for change is just around the corner, in someone you meet, on a page of a book or in a moment of self-reflection.

As the author of 93 books myself, you can imagine how fussy I am to write a foreword to publications in the business and self-development space. My friend Jim Britt is an exception. He has spent decades influencing millions of individuals with his many best-selling books, seminars, programs and coaching, to blossom into the best version of themselves. He has the knowledge, wisdom and skillsets needed to make a significant contribution to overcoming issues entrepreneurs face in business today. His success speaks for itself.

In a world where the pursuit of wealth and success often dominates our collective consciousness, the concept of cracking the rich code has become an elusive quest for many. We marvel at the seemingly effortless success stories of millionaires and billionaires, wondering what secret knowledge or hidden talents they possess that have propelled them to riches. Yet, behind every success story lies a unique and inspiring journey, woven with challenges, triumphs, and invaluable lessons learned.

It is with great excitement that I present to you "Cracking the Rich Code," a book that unveils the remarkable successes of 20 millionaire coauthors. These individuals have not only achieved extraordinary success, but have also generously shared their insights, strategies, and wisdom, inviting the readers to embark on their own transformative journeys.

Within these pages you will discover a variety of stories that defy the myth of an easily attainable overnight success. Instead, you will discover stories of resilience, determination and the unrelenting decisions to pursue their dreams. Each author offers a unique perspective on wealth creation, sharing the secrets they unlocked along their path to financial success.

As you read each chapter you will encounter diverse backgrounds, highlighting the fact that the rich code is not for a certain gender, race, age or social status. You will discover that there are a myriad of ways in which financial success can be achieved.

So, prepare to be inspired as you witness the transformative power of perseverance and the unwavering belief in one's abilities. Through their stories, each coauthor will take you behind the scenes of their successes, allowing you a glimpse into the countless hours of hard work, sacrifices, and failures they encountered along the way.

This book is not just about destination; it's about the journey. Beyond the accumulation of wealth, these authors emphasize the importance of personal growth, finding purpose, and making a positive impact on the world. They share their experience of self-discovery and self-improvement, and offer guidance on developing the mindset, habits, and values necessary to build sustainable success in any and all areas of life.

Their stories will reveal that the rich code is not a hidden secret, but rather a blueprint for anyone willing to embrace the principles with dedication and perseverance. It's about learning from failures, embracing risks, overcoming fears, and continuously expanding one's knowledge and skills. It's about having a mindset of abundance, nurturing relationships, and giving back to society.

Whether you are an aspiring entrepreneur, a seasoned professional, or simply seeking inspiration and guidance, "Cracking the Rich Code" will provide a roadmap to unlocking your real potential. Through the diverse perspectives of Jim Britt and the coauthors, you will find a wealth of actionable strategies, that will empower you to rewrite your own story and chart your course toward financial prosperity.

Let's help in this quest, as Jim Britt and the talented coauthors unselfishly donate their most important asset, their precious LIFETIME of experience, to elevate one life at a time to their full potential and greatness.

If I were you, I would buy 10, and then giftwrap them to acknowledge your most important top ten relationships in life or clients in business. By doing so, you will strengthen the relationship and encourage others to live a more fulfilling life.

As you close the pages of any of the books in this series, you will gain a new life of clarity and focus as never before. *Cracking the Rich Code* will provide tools to transform results for corporations, institutions, and individuals, both personally and financially.

If you've ever wanted to read a book that challenges you to become more than you are and leaves you with enough inspiration to last a lifetime, *Cracking the Rich Code* is it!

Allow all you have read in this book to create introspection and redirection if required.

Remember, death is certain. Success is not. This life is your journey to craft.

Brian Tracy

Table of Contents

Foreword by Brian Tracy xi

Jim Britt 1
    Think Like Superman

Rory Douglas 13
    The Money Game: Millennial Makeover

Gabriella Alziari 19
    From Consulting to Consciousness

Hylke Faber 29
    Connectedness Quotient:Committing to What is Most Important to You

Jim Carbaugh 39
    There is a Lesson to LEARN in Every Story

Angilie Kapoor 51
    Beyond Myth and Fiction: The Truth About the Hero's Journey

Sir James Gray Robinson, Esq 63
    Establishing Yourself as a Luxury Brand

Judy Copenbarger 71
    So, You're in Business.... Now What?

Dona Kappmeyer 83
    When I Grow Up?

Mark Yuzuik 91
    Can't Hypnotize Me, I'm Smart and Strong Willed._LOL, Yeah Right

Markiesha E. Wilson 101

Give more. The Surprising Answer to Life's Big Questions

Ryan Lombardo 111

Cracking the Rich Code: The Power of Health Optimization

Princess Merrilee of Solana Ph.D 123

To Love and Be Loved in Return

Deena Giordano Ullom 133

Awakening the Giant: A Journey Beyond Limiting Beliefs

Carole Stizza 143

From Adversity to Advantage: Redefining Your Leadership Story

Steve Walsh 153

Breaking into Management

Phillip Suggs 161

Pandora's Box A Guide to Consumer-Centric Selling

Cecelia "Fi" Mazanke 173

The World's Richest Shoeshine Man

Jim Diebold 183

How Effective is Your Sales Process

John Verrico 193

The Enrichment of Change

Helen Kagan 203

Authenticity. Comfort Zone. Integrity. Success. Our "new normal"?

Afterword 215

Jim Britt

Jim Britt is an award-winning author of 15 best-selling books and ten #1 International best-sellers. Some of his many titles include Rings of Truth, Do This. Get Rich-For Entrepreneurs, Unleashing Your Authentic Power, The Power of Letting Go, Cracking the Rich Code and The Entrepreneur.

He is an internationally recognized business and life strategist who is highly sought after as a keynote speaker, both online and live, for all audiences.

As an entrepreneur Jim has launched 28 successful business ventures. He has served as a success strategist to over 300 corporations worldwide and is one of the world's top 50 most influential speakers and top 20 life and business success strategists. He was presented with the "Best of the Best" award out of the top 100 contributors of all time to the Direct Selling industry.

For over four decades Jim has presented seminars throughout the world sharing his success strategies and life enhancing realizations with over 5,000 audiences, totaling almost 2,000,000 people from all walks of life.

Early in his speaking career he was Business partners with the late Jim Rohn for eight years, where Tony Robbins worked under Jim's direction for his first few years in the speaking business.

As a performance strategist, Jim leverages his skills and experience as one of the leading experts in peak performance, entrepreneurship and personal empowerment to produce stellar results. He is pleased to work with small business entrepreneurs, and anyone seeking to remove the blocks that stop their success in any area of their life.

One of Jim's latest programs "Cracking the Rich Code" focuses on the subconscious programs influencing one's relationship with money and their financial success. www.CrackingTheRichCode.com

Think Like Superman
By Jim Britt

"Waking up to your true greatness in life requires letting go of who you imagine yourself to be."

--- Jim Britt

FACT: Becoming a millionaire is easier than it has ever been.

Many people have the notion that it's an impossible task to become a millionaire. Some say, "It's pure luck." Others say, "You have to be born into a rich family." For others, "You'll have to win the Lotto." And for many, they say, "Your parents have to help you out a lot." That's the language of the poor.

A single mother with five children says, "I want to believe in what you're saying. However, I'm 45 years old and work long hours at two dead-end jobs. I barely earn enough to get by. What should I do?"

Another man said, "Well, if you work for the government, you cannot expect to become a millionaire. After all, you're on a fixed salary and there's little time for anything else. By the time you get home, you've got to play with the kids, eat dinner, and fall asleep watching TV."

Everyone has a story as to why they could never become a millionaire. But for every story, excuse really, there are other stories OR PEOPLE with worse circumstances that have become rich.

The truth is that all of us can become as wealthy as we decide to be, and that's a mindset. None of us is excluded from wealth. If you have the desire to receive money, whatever the amount, you have all of the rights to do so like everyone else. There is no limit to how much you can earn for yourself. The only limitations are what you place on yourself.

Money is like the sun. It does not discriminate. It doesn't say, "I will not give light and warmth to this flower, tree, or person because I don't like them." Like the sun, money is abundantly available to all of us who truly believe that it is for us. No one is excluded.

There are, however, some major differences between rich and poor people. Here are some tips for becoming rich.

Change Your Thinking

You have to see the bigger picture. There are opportunities everywhere! The problem is that most people see just trees when they should be looking at the entire forest. By doing so, you will see that there are opportunities everywhere. The possibilities are endless.

You'll also have to go through plenty of self-discovery before you earn your first million. Knowing the truth about yourself isn't always the easiest task. Sometimes, you'll find that you are your biggest enemy—at least some days.

Learn from Millionaires

Most people are surrounded by what I like to call their "default friends." These friends are acquaintances that we see at the gym, school, work, local happy hour, and other places. We naturally befriend these people because we are all in the same boat financially. However, these people aren't millionaires in most cases and cannot help you become one either. In fact, if you tell them, you will become a millionaire, some may even tell you that it's impossible and discourage you from even trying. They'll tell you that you're living in a fantasy world and why you'll never be able to make it happen. Instead, learn from millionaires. Let go of these relationships that pull you down regarding your money desires. It's okay to have friends that aren't millionaires. However, only take input from those who have accomplished what you want to accomplish. Hang out with those who will encourage and help you reach the next level. Don't give your raw diamonds to a bricklayer to cut.

Indulge in Wealth

To become wealthy, you must learn about wealth. This means that you'll have to put yourself in situations that you've never been in before.

ON OCCASION, DO SOME OF THESE:

Fly first class and see how it makes you feel.

Eat out at the finest restaurant, and don't look at the price on the menu.

Take a limo instead of a cab or Uber. Watch how you feel.

Reserve a suite in a first-class hotel.

If you are used to drinking a $20 bottle of wine, go for the $100 and see how it tastes. It does taste different.

All I am saying is, try some things that wealthy people do and see how it makes you feel.

Believe it is Possible

If you believe it is possible to become a millionaire, you can make it happen. However, if you've excluded yourself from this possibility and think and believe that it's for other people, you'll never become a millionaire.

Also, be sure to bless rich people when you can. Haters of money aren't likely to receive any of it either.

Read books that millionaires have written. By gaining a well-rounded education about earning large sums of money and staying inspired, you'll be able to learn the wealth secrets of the rich. I just saw a video on LinkedIn with my friend Kevin Harrington from the TV show Shark Tank. He said that one of his new companies just had a million-dollar day on Amazon.

Enlarge Your Service

Your material wealth is the sum of your total contribution to society. Your daily mantra should be, *'How do I deliver more value to more people in less time?'* Then, you'll know that you can always increase your quality and quantity of service. Enlarging your service is also about going the extra mile. When it comes to helping others, you must give everything you have. You just plant the seeds, and nature will take care of the rest.

Seize ALL Opportunities That Make Sense

You cannot say "No" to opportunities and expect to become a millionaire. You must seize every opportunity that has your name on it. It may just be an opportunity to connect with an influential person for no reason. Sometimes the monetary reward will not come immediately, but if you keep planting seeds, eventually, you'll grow a fruitful crop. Money is the harvest of the service you provide and sometimes the connections you have. The more seeds you plant, the greater the harvest.

Have an Unstoppable Mindset

Want to know some of what my first mentor shared with me that took me from a broke factory worker, a high school dropout, to a millionaire?

First, he said, you must start thinking like a wealthy, unstoppable person. You must have a wealth mindset. He said that wealthy people think differently. He said, "I want you to start thinking like Superman!" Sounds crazy, right? Well, it's not. It's powerful, and here's why. How you think and focus on will change your life.

Wealthy people think differently. They really do. And anyone can learn to think like the wealthy.

I'm not talking about positive thinking, the Law of Attraction, or motivation. Let's get real. None of that stuff works anyway. Otherwise, we would all be prosperous and happy already. Instead, I'm talking about thinking based on quantum physics. Once you understand and apply it, it will change your life. You will become unstoppable!

If there was any fictional or real person whose qualities you could instantly possess, who would that person be? Think about it. Personally, I would say that Superman is the perfect person. Now, you are probably thinking I have lost it, right? Just stick with me here. You will like what you are about to hear.

Superman is a fictional superhero widely considered one of the most famous and popular action heroes and an American cultural icon. I remember watching Superman every Saturday morning when I was a kid. I couldn't get enough. He was my hero!

Let's look at Superman's traits:

Superman is indestructible.

He is a man of steel.

He can stop a locomotive in its tracks.

Bullets bounce off him.

He is faster than a speeding bullet.

No one can bring him down.

He can leap tall buildings in a single bound. Great powers to have in this day and age, wouldn't you say? What else would you need?

Now, for all you females, don't worry. We have not left you out. There is also a female version of Superman named Superwoman. She has the same powers as Superman.

Now, this is where it gets interesting. Let's first look at the qualities that Superman possesses that you want to make your own. And to make it simple, I will refer to Superman for the rest of this message, and you can replace him with Superwoman if you are female.

Again:

Superman is powerful and fearless.

Superman is virtually indestructible—except for kryptonite, of course.

Superman can stop bullets.

Superman has supernatural powers. He can see through walls.

Superman can stop a speeding locomotive.

Superman can stop a bullet.

Superman jumps into immediate action when troubles arise.

Superman can crash through barriers.

Superman can even change clothes in a phone booth in seconds. Not too many of those around anymore. You'll have to duck behind a building to change.

So, you're thinking right now, *'Okay, I know that Superman has incredible supernatural powers, how can that help me? What good will it do me to think I am Superman, a fictional character?'*

Here is where science comes in. This is the part where you will be amazed when you learn about the supernatural powers you already possess! NO, REALLY!

Your brain makes certain chemicals called neuropeptides. These are literally the molecules of emotion, like love, fear, joy, passion, etc. These molecules of emotion are not only contained in your brain but circulate throughout your cellular structure. They send out a signal, a frequency much like a radio station sending out a signal. For example, you tune in to 92.5, and you get jazz. Tune in to 99.6, and you get rock. And if you are just one decimal off, you get static. The difference is that your signal goes both ways. You are a sender and a receiver.

You put out a signal, a mindset of confidence about your financial success, and people, circumstances, and opportunities show up to support your success. When you put out a signal of doubt and uncertainty, you receive support for your doubt and uncertainty. You've been around someone you didn't trust or felt less than positive just being in their presence, right? You have also been around people that inspire you. That's what I'm talking about. You are projecting a frequency, looking to resonate with the frequency you are transmitting.

Anyway, the amazing part about these cells of emotion is that they are intelligent. They are thinking cells. These cells are constantly eavesdropping on the conversation that you are having with yourself. That's right. They are listening to you! And others are listening to your cells as well. Others feel what you feel when they are around you.

Your unconscious mind and cells are listening in, waiting to adjust your behavior based on what they hear from you, their master. So just imagine what would happen if you started thinking like Superman or a millionaire.

Here are some of the thoughts you might have during the day:

"The challenges I face today are easily overcome, after all I am Superman."

"I am indestructible."

"I have incredible strength."

"Nothing can stop me...NOTHING."

"I have supernatural powers and can overcome anything."

"I can accomplish anything I want when I put my mind to it."

"I can break through any barrier."

"I can and I will do whatever it takes to accomplish my goal."

"I fear nothing."

The trillions of thinking cells in your body and brain listen, and they create exactly what you tell them to create. Their mission is to complete the picture of the you they see and hear when you talk to them. They must obey. It's their job!

Since you are Superman, you cannot fail. Why? Your thinking cells are now sending the proper signal because you told them to. They are making you stronger and more successful every day! You have the ability to fight off all negativity, doubt, fear, and worry—nothing can stop you!

Superman has total confidence. So, your cells of emotion relating to confidence will now create more neuropeptide chemicals to promote feelings of power and confidence that others will feel in your presence.

Superman is fearless. So, your cells of emotion relating to fear will now create more neuropeptide chemicals to create feelings of courage. You are unstoppable!

And here's the key. Others will respond to you in the same way that you are talking to yourself.

If you are confident, others will have confidence in you.

You have thousands of thoughts every day. Make sure your thoughts are leading you in the direction you want to go. Ensure you tell your cells a success story and not a 'woe is me' story.

Most have been conditioned to think that creating wealth is difficult or only for the lucky few. What do you believe? It doesn't cost anything to think like Superman, and it is much more inspiring!

Mediocrity cannot be an option if you decide to be wealthy and think like Superman.

Your decision and communication with your cells create a mindset; that influences how you show up.

None of that old type of thinking matters anymore. After all, you are Superman, and you can accomplish anything.

If you want wealth, you have to stretch yourself. You have to do the things that unsuccessful people are unwilling to do. You have to say "yes" to an opportunity, then figure out how to get the job done.

Maybe you are uncomfortable selling and asking for money. If that's the case, then learn sales and learn to ask for money every day until you feel comfortable asking for it. You will never have money if you don't learn to ask for it.

I've learned a lot in the past 40+ years as an entrepreneur. I've learned that in order to have more, you have to become more. I've also learned that if you are comfortable, you are not growing. I realized that I couldn't go from being a nervous rookie speaker with minimal self-confidence to hosting TV shows and speaking in front of 5,000 people overnight. I simply wasn't ready. I grew into that, one speaking engagement at a time. Every time I finished a speaking engagement, I would ask myself, "How did I do it, and how could I do it better?" I still do that today.

And I've learned from the hundreds of thousands of people I've trained, coached, and mentored that none of us can do something we don't believe is possible. It won't happen if you're not ready to step out of your comfort zone and stretch yourself.

This has led me to understand the most important principle of wealth-building, which has meant the difference between poverty and riches for people since humans first traded for pelts.

Are you ready?

Come in just a little closer. Listen up!

Every income level requires a different you, a different mindset! If you think that $10,000 a month is a lot of money, then $100,000 a month will be completely out of reach. If you believe that having $5,000 in the bank would make you rich, then $50,000 won't miraculously appear. You will never earn more money than you believe is "a lot" of money.

What you do as a business is only a small part of becoming rich. In fact, there are thousands, if not tens of thousands, of ways to make money—and lots of it. I've learned over the years that focusing on who you want to become instead of what you need to do will multiply your chances of getting rich a hundredfold.

Ask anyone who's found a way to make a large sum of money legally, and they will tell you that it's not hard once you crack the code. And cracking the code starts with you and your mindset. The "code" I refer to isn't a secret rite or ancient scroll. It's not even a secret. It's a certain way of thinking and believing in which you've trained your mind to see money-making ideas.

That's where you see a need in the marketplace and jump on the idea quickly. It might involve creating a new product, or it may just be teaching others a special technique you've learned. It may even require raising capital to start a company or to market a product or idea on social media.

Don't Hold Back. You Have to Take Action to Change.

Start right now to imagine yourself as already having wealth. How would your life be? How would your day unfold? Start to own your wealth mindset now! The subconscious mind is unable to differentiate between fact and mere visualization. So, by imagining that you already have it, you're encouraging your subconscious mind to seek the ways and means to transform your imaginary feelings into the real thing.

Find yourself some mentors. Nobody has all the answers. Surround yourself with people who will support, inspire, and provide solutions that keep you moving in the right direction. Having a qualified mentor is essential if you genuinely want to attain wealth, have a thriving business, or reach the top of your game in any endeavor.

Okay, let's come in for a landing…

Having a crystal-clear picture of what you want to accomplish is essential before you begin. If you want to attain wealth, you must learn to operate without fear and with a sharply defined mental image of the outcome you want to attain. This comes from thinking like a wealthy person (like Superman), making decisions like a wealthy person, and being fearless (like Superman) when stepping out of your comfort zone. Look at the result as something you're already prepared to do; you just haven't done it yet.

Think about this. You have been preventing your success; it's not something you have to struggle to make happen. The key is not letting fear, doubt, other people, or mind chatter push your success away. You'll find that the solutions taking you toward your goals will come to you in the most unexpected and sudden ways. You don't need the *perfect* plan first. You need a perfectly clear decision about your success, the right mindset, mentoring, and the ideal way to get you there will materialize.

The most significant transfer of wealth in the history of the human race is happening right now. Are you positioned to get your share?

Remember, in order to get a different result, you must do something different. In order to do something different, you must know something different to do. And in order to know something different, you have to first suspect that your present methods need improving.

THEN, YOU HAVE TO BE WILLING TO DO SOMETHING ABOUT IT.

***

To contact Jim:

For more information on Jim's work:

www.JimBritt.com

http://JimBrittCoaching.com

www.facebook.com/jimbrittonline

www.linkedin.com/in/jim-britt

For free audio series sessions 1&2 www.PowerOfLettingGo.com

Rory Douglas

Rory Douglas is a Best-Selling Author, Financial Educator and High-Performance Life Coach. He was born in Chicago, IL and raised in Los Angeles CA. Moving to Los Angeles, Douglas made his mark in the music industry by developing his company, RKD Music & Talent Management, with his former law partner Joseph Gellman.

Douglas has over 20 years' experience in the Entertainment and Investment industry empowering entrepreneurs to pursue their purpose. He transitioned from Entertainment to the Financial Services industry where he leads and mentors' countless amount of people including CEOs, CPA, Attorneys and several seven figure earners who run their own organizations. He has built several millionaires and counting. "The average American is 1 to 2 paychecks away from being homeless and 1 and 3 are in debt", says Douglas who is traveling all around the world speaking with Youth & Community Organizations, Colleges and Universities, Corporations as well as Ministries and Non-Profits.

Douglas is also Author of books like **"Artificial Intelligence"**, **"The Power to Get Wealth: No Money Required"** and the Best-Selling book **"Fear to Freedom"**. He has quickly become a force in the financial industry as well as a leading authority on retirement planning as a Financial Educator and Retirement Specialist.

Douglas is on a National Financial Literacy Campaign to educate 1 million families each year. His firm, Aqua Financial Center, is in Woodland Hills, CA.

The Money Game: Millennial Makeover
By Rory Douglas

There is a Grave Epidemic that is going on in America today. The average American is at least one to two paychecks away from being homeless; one in three are in debt. The average American cannot handle a $400 emergency and millennials have zero savings.

Millennials having zero savings is very troubling. If this matter is not addressed immediately, the future seems very unfavorable. Also known as Generation Y, millennials are the demographic cohort following Generation X and preceding Generation Z. Researchers and popular media use the early 1980's to the early 2000's as ending birth years, with 1981 to 1996 being a widely accepted definition.

A millennial makeover is when someone does not see their full potential. They need someone else to come in and show them the way. According to recent surveys, North American's are facing serious financial challenges. Thirty-three percent, or more than 77-million Americans don't pay their bills on time. Thirty-nine percent carry credit card debt from month to month. Only 59% percent of adults say they have savings. Worse, more than half now think it's acceptable to default on their mortgage if they can't afford to pay.

Many of us don't wait to become a statistic to know that we're in trouble. These problems are all around us. They happen to be in our own families and friends. It's ironic that we live in one of the wealthiest countries in the world, but we always have money problems. We can work hard all of our lives but retire poorly. So much effort we put into providing a bright future for our kids just to see them finish college buried in debt.

Debt becomes a way of life. Nobody teaches us how to manage our money in school. Financial issues are not often discussed; financial products are not always explained. Most people have trouble balancing their own check books and reading a financial statement. Credit cards are used daily without a clear understanding of hidden charges. We contribute to our retirement plans with the hope that someone else will grow it. People don't plan to fail; they just fail to have a plan.

Millennials must get prepared for a new industry. Artificial intelligence will create major job displacements. Trouble is on the horizon. Today, we go into the supermarket, bank, airport, parking lots, and we see machines. Students must be aware of the dangers and pitfalls that lie ahead.

According to the McKinsey Global Institute, up to 800-million global workers will lose their jobs by 2030 and be replaced by robotic automation. Some of the jobs that will soon become extinct are newspaper workers, travel agents, radio jockeys, bank tellers, truck drivers and manufacturing workers.

Financial literacy is a must. Millennials must learn how to take care of their financial selves or prepare to suffer the consequences. Vast amounts of millennials are training for a career that is fading away as a new industry is coming in. It is imperative that the information that is right under the noses of millennials is brought to their attention. It's just like a tree, if you don't like the fruit that the tree produces, don't get mad at the fruit, get mad at the root.

Although education is key, millennials must allow their imaginations to run wild and pursue their purpose through entrepreneurship and creativity. Millennials must get their SHIFT together and quickly. This new industry requires a new mindset. Independence and entrepreneurism are needed like never before. Today in America, a new home-based business is started every twelve-seconds. Did you know that home-based businesses earn $427 billion a year? It is estimated that in the United States, there are 38-million home-based businesses. Seventy percent of home-based businesses succeed within three years vs regular businesses. Forty-four percent of home-based businesses are started for under $5,000. Twenty percent of home-based businesses make $100,000 to $500,000 a year. Eighty-five percent of Americans are dissatisfied with their job. Over 70% of Americans would prefer to be self-employed.

Now it's time for millennials to get into the money game and crack the rich code. Let's start with the real rate of return on our money. The average major bank in America gives us, on average, about a minus one percent interest on a checking or savings account. We have more than 13-trillion-dollars sitting in United States banks earning less than 1% interest. Inflation is about 3.5%. For example, if you saved $100 at 3% interest that would yield you $103.00. The taxes on $103.00 is about 75 cents. Net after taxes is $102.25. The inflation is $3.50. The actual return is $98.75, so you lose.

Would you rather pay $0.75 or $3.50? Quite naturally you would rather pay $0.75 but I have news for you, we pay both. It's not the taxes that's killing us, it's inflation, which I call the silent killer. We must have at least 5% or greater interest to beat taxes and inflation.

The second component is The Rule of 72 and compounding interest. The Rule of 72 is used by all banking institutions and finance companies. The Rule of 72 can work for you or against you. It works for you if you are receiving interest. However, if you are paying interest, like a credit card, it works against you.

Want this formula? Simply take the number 72 and divide it into any rate of return. That tells you how long it takes to double your money. The two above statements are examples of the failure of the educational system. Schools do not teach us how to sell, think, negotiate, face our failures, invest our money, find our passion, make an impact, start a business, or how to communicate well.

In fact, the conditions of the millennials today have a substantial resemblance to the Great Depression. For example, during the great depression, Americans suffered a massive job loss, lack of opportunity, collapse of major job industries, and collapse of the stock market. These conditions left Americans with scarce liquidity and very little to transfer to the succeeding generation. Americans had to use life insurance as a form of wealth transformation.

Wealth transformation is the transfer of wealth or assets to beneficiaries upon the death of the owner through financial planning. These strategies often include wills, estate planning, life insurance, or trusts. Although today's conditions in America are polar opposite of that during the Great Depression, due to financial illiteracy and the millennials having zero savings, they must use the same resources as did their predecessors for financial freedom. Today's society is filled with booming industries, technological advancements, social media, and abundant opportunities. Unfortunately, millennials have no form of wealth transformation.

Frankly, they have nothing to transfer. If millennials don't shift their thinking, perilous times lie ahead.

I believe today's millennials are the finest that America has yet to see. They are fearless, creative, resourceful and highly educated. They simply need to crack the rich code by understanding the importance of financial literacy and entrepreneurism. If they do, they will be unstoppable, and the future looks very promising.

Take a look at some of the top industries and who's leading the way. For example, Mark Zuckerberg of Facebook, Travis Kalanick and Garrett Camp of Uber, Brian Chesky of Airbnb, Ben Silbermann and Evan Sharp of Pinterest, Adam D'Angelo of Quora, Mike Krieger and Kevin Systrom of Instagram and Sean Rad of Tinder to name a few. The millennials above have managed to disrupt and revolutionize the way we approach travel, socializing and even dating. They are prime examples of what happens when millennials think outside of the box.

Now that we all are motivated after reading that list, I have a few suggestions for millennials to take while they are encompassing their entrepreneurial ventures: They must establish a solid foundation (i.e., having a form of wealth transformation such as life insurance). They must establish a debt management plan (i.e. raising their credit score). They must apply the "10/20 Rule" (They need at least ten-times their monthly expenses saved up for an emergency and at least twenty-times their yearly salary to retire). Remember, retirement has nothing to do with your age. You can retire at 18-years-old if you're financially secure. Lastly, once the foundation is secure, they can invest. Millennials today invest first, save last, and have no foundation. Furthermore, millennials have to transition from flat interest to compounding interest, and they must learn about the three forms of taxes to get ahead.

The three forms of taxes are tax now, tax later, and tax advantage. The average American is in the tax now category which are checking accounts, savings accounts, CD's, stocks and mutual funds. Following that is the tax later category which are 401k's, IRA's, annuities and pensions. We must get into the tax advantage (tax free) category which are Roth IRA's, college savings plans, municipal bonds, health savings accounts and life insurance. We can no longer have a champagne taste with a beer budget.

I would encourage millennials to take full advantage of the unlimited opportunities that are available today. Always remember that opportunity and access is greater than money. We have to remove ourselves from the mentality of trading time for money and the rat race of the 9-5. Start thriving as opposed to surviving. Don't be discouraged as success is often found in a pile of mistakes. Do not allow your circumstances to shrink your dreams and most certainly do not allow fear to rob you of your destiny. If millennials combine their faith, belief and passion with their education, financial literacy, and entrepreneurism, they will have money for a lifetime and not just a lunch time.

***

To contact Rory:

www.RorykDouglas.co

info@rorykdougas.com

Phone: (747) 224-0706

Instagram: RorykDouglas

Tiktok: RoryDouglasOfficial

Facebook: OfficialRoryDouglas

Youtube: OfficialRoryDouglas

Gabriella Alziari

Gabriella Alziari is a highly sought-after Intuitive Channeler, Life Coach and Entrepreneur with over 100,000 social media followers and an impressive client list that includes Hollywood celebrities, CEOs, and authors in over 50 countries. Her ability to combine behavioral coaching with intuitive insights has helped countless individuals attain clarity, achieve their goals, and manifest their dreams.

Gabriella's discovery of her intuitive gifts began shortly after she completed a Master's Degree in Organizational Behavior from the London School of Economics and entered the corporate world as a Leadership Coach. Honing her craft, Gabriella's success as a Spirit Guide Reader on her YouTube and Instagram channels was so undeniable that she eventually transitioned to spiritual work full-time. She offers uniquely resonant readings that guide her clients to access a flow state in which the answers they need can be found.

Leveraging her business background, Gabriella is also in high demand as a Life Coach for business owners and entrepreneurs, helping them achieve personal and professional outcomes based on a deepened intuitive understanding. Her six-month coaching program helps individuals harness their own intuitive capabilities and build the life of their dreams.

Looking for guidance on a business or personal decision — or simply seeking more confidence, fulfillment, and success? Connect with Gabriella and take the next steps to access your intuition, discover your purpose, and accelerate your success.

From Consulting to Consciousness
By Gabriella Alziari

My God, has it really been two hours?

I just reread the email for what must have been the hundredth time and glanced at my desk clock.

Yep. It was a quarter to eight in the morning when I first sat down, intending to give the resignation email I'd drafted the previous evening one last read-through before pushing "send." It was now half past nine. What should have taken ten minutes tops had taken ten times that, as the morning's initial wave of nervousness had swelled into a paralysis of fear. Of giving up a secure job. Of change. Of failure. What if I had misjudged my own potential?

I closed my eyes and inhaled deeply, letting my mind settle in the moments that followed. Then, I exhaled the fear along with the soft slip of my breath.

Gabriella, you need to do this. Do it for yourself. Do it for your community.

I pressed send.

With a simple touch of my finger, seven years as a high-performance leadership coach and consultant came to an end.

Gabriella Alziari's reboot was complete.

Drawn to the Ethereal

The seeds of this personal revolution had been sown many years earlier, long before I embraced the competitiveness of the corporate world. In my childhood I had been wildly creative, fascinated with artistic pursuits and mystical explorations.

From the age of 10, I had been drawn to books on meditation, consciousness, energy healing, past life regression—basically anything that dared to challenge societal conventions regarding our experience of the material world. Looking back, I realize those early fascinations reflected more than a rebellious skepticism toward 'authoritative' explanations: I was hungry to uncover the root causes of phenomena, causes that most people seemed too ready to overlook. I was, by nature, an explorer.

But something happened as I got older. Although I never fully lost the desire to understand the mysteries of the human experience, that curiosity was redirected by the pressures of emerging adulthood. I found myself taking a more conventional route. In 2018, freshly minted with a Master's degree in Organizational Behavior from the London School of Economics, I entered the corporate world of emails, conference calls, reports, deadlines and all the rest. As a leadership coach and consultant in this high-pressure environment, I excelled. And yet . The entire time I was succeeding in the corporate world, I never quite felt at ease in my corporate identity. I would sit on calls, feeling a heaviness in my chest. Eventually, I began to dread going to work each day. Something was clearly off.

Then in 2020, the pandemic hit—and with it, I felt the malaise of being confined at home with too much time on my hands. One day, on a whim to stave off boredom, I decided to revisit my childhood passion and began studying tarot cards. I mastered all 78 cards, learning every symbol, astrological representation and meaning. It was deeply satisfying. Before long, I began offering readings to my friends and family members. To my genuine surprise and initial bafflement, one by one they began informing me that my readings were coming true.

When eventually more than 20 separate people assured me there was validity to my readings, I decided to up the stakes and I started a YouTube channel to share my work. The night I posted my first video, I remember telling myself, *If this video gets 40 views by the time I wake up tomorrow, I'll dedicate myself to this channel.*

The next morning, the video had 42 views.

Pleased with this result, I began my new vocation with entrepreneurial enthusiasm, posting at least one video per week. Eventually, my channel reached over 50,000 subscribers.

The Plot Thickens

The contrast I felt between this spiritual work and my continuing corporate career was striking.

When doing readings, my spirit was light and joyful—unlike the passionless drudgery of my corporate work.

Additionally, the comments I received on my YouTube channel were amazing. Complete strangers affirmed that I was psychic—the real deal—with comments like "How on earth did you know that?" and "Your reading was so accurate, you must've put cameras in my house!"

Strangely enough, these comments reminded me of feedback I often received as a corporate leadership coach. Clients would say, "Wow, I can't believe you understand my situation so well. It's uncanny." I had always chalked this up to being a great listener, but I began to realize I'd been drawing all this time on a deep intuition that was now manifesting itself in eerily accurate tarot readings as well.

The more I puzzled over this growing body of evidence, the more compelled I felt to conclude that—as many spiritual researchers have long claimed—energy transcends time and space in a way that has so far eluded traditional science. Was it possible I had been connecting to the consciousness of my family, friends, YouTube viewers, and even corporate clients, accessing accurate information about their lives via my intuition?

I might still have dismissed all this if it hadn't been for the fact that, around this time, sets of seemingly random images would spontaneously flash in my mind, one after another, while doing readings. When I shared this with my YouTube viewers, it turned out that the images held great significance for some of them, representing important moments and decisions they faced in their lives. I learned this is called "clairvoyance": the ability to see with your mind's eye. On multiple occasions, my viewers told me that the images and messages I shared were uncannily accurate—some even belonging to lost loved ones.

Letting the Market Lead

Ironically, in December 2019, just months before I launched my YouTube channel, I had incorporated my business with the aim of establishing my own corporate coaching firm. Yet, despite receiving rave reviews from my initial clients, I struggled to find the high-ticket clients I would need for the business to succeed. The sudden onset of COVID wasn't helping. I found myself putting in substantial amounts of time with little to no reward.

Meanwhile, my growing YouTube channel presented the opposite problem: I could hardly keep up with the requests pouring in. The contrast between the heaviness of the corporate world and the lightness I felt helping people find clarity was unmistakable. For so many years I'd tried to do what I *thought* I was meant to do, mastering every role and assignment given to me. But all that followed from these successes was second-guessing myself for being "different". I had been pressing my naturally creative spirit into the mold of an environment that suppressed the greatest gift I possessed: my intuition.

Now, I had the chance to break free of the mold. I embraced my new identity as an Intuitive and added Reiki training to my growing spiritual repertoire. I resolved to learn everything I could about energy and intuition. I discovered that I could access my intuition through physical sensations like shivers, chills, and tingles (what is called "clairsentience"). I started to listen to my body in a way I never had before, doing daily exercises to become more aware of the state of my heart and gut, finding wisdom there just as important as that of the mind. I withdrew from people-pleasing tendencies and learned to commit only to what aligns with my Soul.

The result was a happier, healthier me, more in touch with my desires and with who I am at my core. I realized that the feelings of density I encountered during my 9-to-5 indicated that the conventional corporate dream was not my path. Among spiritual practitioners, this feeling of constriction is regarded as an intuitive "no"—indicating that something isn't in alignment with your Soul. The light, expansive feeling I experienced when doing spiritual work was my body's "yes!"

Within months, I updated my services to offer a variety of spiritual sessions: readings, energy healing, life coaching, and intuitive development. Increasingly, my devotion to spiritual coaching was taking precedence over my other professional activities. I remember being on coaching calls with my corporate clients, feeling the immense stress and tension they were experiencing, and thinking to myself, *wow, this person would really benefit from Reiki.*

I decided to let the market lead and poured myself into the spiritual work I loved, building up a loyal following, receiving recognition on a global scale, and generating far more business than I had expected. Client after client, technique after technique, session after session, I mastered my craft. I developed my own method of combining behavioral coaching and intuition, with the goal of helping others understand their true purpose.

I watched as my clients completely transformed their lives: leaving jobs that didn't align with them to start their own businesses, moving across the world to pursue new opportunities, and even writing articles that were featured in the New York Times. It was amazing to witness them achieve what they used to believe was out of reach.

The Reboot

This brings me back to that day when the above culminated in one touch of a finger—the moment I stepped off the corporate path and dedicated myself to my true path all along. That path had always been there waiting for me. I just needed time to learn how to hear my inner voice and, most importantly, trust it.

Not to imply it was an easy decision to make. Many of the people I had relied on for stability tried to dissuade me from going full-time into spiritual work. "It's just too risky," they would say. Their words caused me to question myself and try to throw myself 'all in' to my corporate job.

But it just wasn't 'me' anymore.

I also sought advice from a group of like-minded peers and spiritual coaches. They never failed to tell me how incredibly talented I am. In one conversation, my friend simply stared at me and said, "The Universe is just waiting for you to do this full-time." There was something in the way she said it that made everything seem suddenly simple. What if the only thing standing in my way all along had been … me?

So, I pushed "send." In the following months, I discovered a stronger belief in myself, more time for rest, more abundance, and, yes, more money. My attitude became "Watch me succeed!" And I did—step by step, trusting my intuition.

I am now, fully and unreservedly, Gabriella Alziari, Intuitive Channeler, Life Coach and Entrepreneur.

Lessons Worth Learning

These experiences have taught me that we have the power to design our dream life, but it takes intention and commitment. Consistency is one of the most important tenets of being a successful entrepreneur. Many people give up on their dreams right before they're about to succeed.

The key to creating external success is to begin with your own internal belief system, where energy expresses itself. It requires dedication to get to the root causes of unhelpful thinking patterns and release them, but if you do the inner work and change your subconscious beliefs, they begin to work for you rather than against you.

Let me share some of the most important lessons I've learned in my journey so far. Perhaps you can draw inspiration from them as well.

Your Soul already knows your path.

You have all the knowledge, wisdom and answers you need already inside you. I know that may sound trite, but I can't stress enough the importance of this fundamental truth. Your own intuitive knowing is more powerful than anything you'll read in a book or buy online. Commit to trusting yourself.

Receiving is as important as doing.

Our society programs us to be in a constant "doing" mode. To access your latent intuition, you'll need to grasp the energy of receiving, which means opening yourself up. What does this look like? Meditating, writing, creating art, running . . . the particular manifestations are up to you.

The important thing is to do these activities uninterrupted, without distractions. This allows you to access a "flow state" in which intuition becomes fully accessible. All great innovations stem from this state.

Learn the difference between Ego, Brain and Intuition.

The Ego is a self-judgment machine. It constantly tells you that you're unworthy—even when things are going well! If you get promoted, your Ego will whisper that you're not up to the job.

The best way to escape the Ego's prison of insecurity is to recognize such thoughts when they arise, label them as the Ego, then put them aside. Ego, I hear you, but I'm choosing not to listen to you.

The Brain is like a computer. You input a task; it spits out a result. It's neither positive nor negative. It simply does what you tell it to do.

Intuition is your true inner knowing. It's the seat of your Soul, where all knowledge, wisdom and answers are available. It's the quiet voice that tells you "Just do it!"—sometimes, even when a decision might seem crazy on the surface. Intuition will let you know what risks to take and investments to make. Learn to distinguish the voice of intuition from that of your Ego and from the voices of other people echoing in your head. If you master this, you'll never be led astray.

Leverage the power of choice.

Each decision you make is not just conscious; it is powered by energy. For this reason, you have the ability to change your external reality through internal alignment. Think back on the big changes of your life: you'll likely find they each emanated from one or more powerful choices. In my case, it was choosing to dedicate myself to my YouTube channel, and later, to trust my intuition and leave my corporate job—despite what many people were telling me. Use your choices wisely. They are your most powerful currency.

It's not possible to become a successful entrepreneur without choosing to step away from the limbo of self-questioning. Don't allow yourself to question the decisions that feel right in your Soul. You know what is true for you. Make a conscious choice and stick to it. Ultimately, this is the difference between living life on your own terms and spending the rest of your life living for someone else.

I'll admit that when I finally chose to leave the corporate world, many of my fears immediately surfaced. I silenced them initially only by sheer will. In time, however, I learned that if you stand firm in your decisions, your Soul will quickly course correct. External reality is more malleable than most of us have been taught to believe. Life isn't a one-item menu. It's a *buffet*, with multiple delicious possibilities available to us as we pass through the line. It's up to you to deliberately choose your path. As you do, let your dreams be bigger than your fears.

Questions Worth Considering

If you're an aspiring entrepreneur, ask yourself:

- What is the highest vision I'm holding for myself?
- Do I truly believe I can achieve it? If not, why?
- What decisions am I making now that will allow this vision to be realized in the future?
- Who are my supporters, the ones there to help hold the vision with me?

If you can identify a clear vision that manifests who you truly are and find a community who'll support you as you transform that vision into reality, your path is set.

Finding your community is crucial. It takes immense courage to walk a path that may be unknowable to many around you. Moments of self-doubt are inevitable. But in those times, you can seek support from a community who believes in your talent and potential. If you make deliberate decisions, show up consistently, and have outside support, there's no way you won't be successful.

Despite the skepticism I faced when I left my corporate career, I have no regrets for making the leap. Today, at 31, I'm a full-time entrepreneur who has built a business that brings me joy and will support me for life. If I can do it, so can you.

Get in Touch

Through Alziari Coaching, I offer a six-month coaching program (including readings) to activate your intuition and help you identify your purpose and vision. Every client who has taken my program has seen immense changes in their life, including a relaxed schedule, enriched relationships, and greater monetary success.

I also host on-stage speaking engagements to teach about the principles of energy, how to make more conscious choices, and finding your life purpose.

I'd be honored to serve as a catalyst in your journey to becoming a more intuitive, successful entrepreneur.

***

To contact Gagriella:

Website:
Alziari Coaching
https://www.alziari.co/
LinkedIn:
Gabriella Alziari
https://www.linkedin.com/in/gabriellaalziari/
YouTube:
Spirituality with Gabriella
https://www.youtube.com/@SpiritualitywithGabriella/videos
Instagram:
@spiritualitygabriella
https://www.instagram.com/spiritualitygabriella/

Hylke Faber

What life is about?

For as long as I can remember, I have contemplated this question. My inquiry has become my work: helping people individually and collectively connect more deeply to what is truly important to them.

I started my work life as a consultant with Towers Perrin and as a Partner with Strategic Decisions Group. I became a 16-hours-a-day consultant and was burning out fast. When I discovered meditation, everything changed.

I realized that there is peace, love and wisdom inside each of us and made it my work to help people thrive by connecting to this magnificent source.

I learned coaching and transformational facilitation, completing my coaching certification with Newfield Network. I applied my learnings at Axialent, cofounded the leadership development company Co-Creation Partners and taught coaching at Columbia Business School Executive Education. I now lead the culture and team development consultancy, Growth Leaders Network.

My writing has appeared in Forbes and Harvard Business Review, and my award-winning book *Taming Your Crocodiles: Unlearn Fear & Become A True Leader* was accolated as one of Bloomberg's 10 best books on leadership for 2018. My next book, *The Connectedness Quotient*, will be published in 2025.

When I'm not coaching leaders and teams, I enjoy singing, hiking, reading, writing and working on personal development. I integrate all of what I learn in my work with executives.

Connectedness Quotient:
Committing to What is Most Important to You
By Hylke Faber

How do you start your day? Most of us have been conditioned to react to whatever shows up on the screens of our minds – the latest challenge, emotional upheaval, bad or good news. Are your inbox, messages, and to-do list the immediate focus of your attention?

We don't have to be like wind vanes, spun about by every passing breeze. We become more impactful, fulfilled, and trusted leaders by intentionally focusing on what is most important – an orientation that distinguishes great leaders from good ones.

Great leaders take time to center themselves before they enter the rest of their world. They are deeply connected to what is most important in themselves, others, and their purpose and lead from that deeper intelligence. I call it Connectedness Quotient, or CQ.

CQ transcends rational intellect (IQ) and emotional intelligence (EQ). Leaders with a high CQ heed an inner call to look beyond their thoughts and feelings and connect to something vast, deep, generous, uplifting, magnificent, wise, and compassionate – in each of us. We can call it presence, awareness, love, and peace, although words don't quite describe it.

Connectedness is available to us always, unaffected by the goings-on of our day-to-day life. Authentically connected leaders tap into CQ by appreciating the essence of what we all are: Something always and already.

Three Connectedness Anchors

How do we develop CQ? Having worked with leaders, teams, and – most importantly – myself for the past two decades, I have observed three core Connectedness Anchors we can apply to build CQ:

- Connect to Self (I): We may give ourselves time and space to meditate, pray, exercise, write, make art, or be in nature before we start our day. We ask ourselves: How present am I now on a scale from 1-10? How can I get closer to 10, where I am utterly present, right here, right now? We may reflect on our values by considering: what is most important to me? Contemplating who we truly are and what we *really* care about helps us connect to the **Truthful Presence** inside ourselves. My values are truth, love, and service. So, I ask myself, "how can I be more truthful, loving, and of service today?"

- Connect to Others (We): We reflect on the people around us. How can we grow closer to them? How can we be more curious, compassionate, and caring? What judgments do we need to let go of? What do they care about? What would life be like in their shoes? This is **Unconditional Empathy**: being open to the feelings and thoughts of others, no matter what, without getting enmeshed in them.

- Connect to Task (It): What actions are called for? What is our real purpose here? What are various ways of working toward our purpose today? Importantly, what are we not to do? How do we avoid getting lost in small-minded, myopic thinking, driven by egocentricity, and let the wisdom of a more integrated viewpoint in? We practice **Vast Purposefulness**, embracing both the vastness of the bigger picture and possibilities in front of us and choosing to do our part today with intention.

How do we practice these three connectedness anchors in our day-to-day lives? Let's explore a personal example.

I am working with a client on a team leadership workshop that is scheduled to take place six weeks from now. I have sent several emails to the team leader, let's call her Mimi, and she hasn't responded. I notice my anxiety. What is going to happen? How will I ensure the workshop goes well if we don't have adequate time to prepare? Does she still want to do it? I have blocked time on my calendar, and if we don't do this, I want to make the time available for other clients. I have a business to run!

Three Wisdom Disconnectors

I notice I am disconnecting from my three Connectedness Anchors – I, We, and It – blinded by the mind-swirl of three common Wisdom

Disconnectors: *Obsessing* (disconnect from I), *Judging* (disconnect from We), and *Controlling* (disconnect from the It, the flow of things and the true task).

I obsess about what will happen, ruminating on nightmare scenarios. I don't feel peace and lose perspective. I am annoyed with Mimi. I judge her. Why can't she cooperate as we agreed!? Frankly, I find it irresponsible! Nowhere in this stream of thinking is any compassion or care for Mimi. And I am starting to think about how I can force a solution to get to the outcome I want, while I know full well that forcing anything just doesn't work.

What is the alternative?

Choosing to return to what is truly important by practicing the three Connectedness Anchors: truthful presence, unconditional empathy, and vast purposefulness.

Truthful Presence: We Are Enough Already

At the beginning of every coaching session and workshop, I ask myself: How present am I now, on a scale from 1-10? I ask again. And again.

What happens with your level of presence when you consciously focus on it? Yes, it increases. Think of presence as the background of our experience, like the sky. The images of our thoughts and feelings appear and disappear on it like clouds. We become quieter as we rest our attention on this skylike presence. We focus on being in the present and notice we are able to loosen our attachments to what we want and lessen our aversion to what we don't want. We are simply here and aware.

Looking through the eyes of presence at Mimi, a wider perspective emerges. Her not responding is no longer an insurmountable obstacle but rather an event – something I can observe and detach from, like a cloud in the sky. I feel grounded in the presence that is already and always here. Nothing has been lost, and nothing real can be gained. I experience the richness of this moment.

I realize I am enough, and so is she, whether we ever work together again or not. We always were enough. The poet Walt Whitman calls this our "unfailing sufficiency." We connect with something constant in us that transcends our actions, thoughts, and feelings, which are as fleeting as clouds. The beingness, presence, love, and peace that we are remains and is always. We can rest here.

From this quieter place, more insight emerges. What is truly important to me? I become ready to listen to my deeper self, which is much wiser than my surface thinking will ever be.

I recall I care about truth, love, and service. How do I live my values now?

Practicing truth, I first deeply accept our mutual enough-ness. I accept that Mimi hasn't responded. I honestly can't know what will happen next. It's my job to be accepting of that and inquire into myself about what I am called to do next. Maybe I should send her another email without obsessing about whether she responds or not. It's not my job to make her respond.

What about practicing love and service? Enter the other two Connectedness Anchors.

Unconditional Empathy: Taming the Judgment Crocodile

How do I become more loving toward Mimi? First, I need to let go of any thoughts and feelings that are not loving – these pesky judgments of the other. My judgmental mind makes Mimi out to be untrustworthy, selfish, and short-sighted. She should respond; if she doesn't, she isn't worthy of my trust. How selfish of her! Didn't we have an agreement?! Doesn't she realize how this unpredictability impacts my work agenda?! Doesn't she realize she is jeopardizing the effectiveness of her team by not taking care of our work together!?

Looking deeper at these judgmental thoughts, I notice they come from a contracted place inside me: a clue that my fight-flight-freeze survival brain is acting up. I call this fearful mind my crocodile, symbolizing the primitive, reactive, reptilian part of our brains that helps us survive.

How do I tame this fearful crocodile? I work with it the way I would work with any anxious child. No, I am not to judge the crocodile for acting up. Of course, it is acting up; that is part of its job. I pause, take a step back from my thinking, and embrace my fear. I extend unconditional kindness to it. I let my crocodile, my reactive inner voice, know I understand it is acting up and accept this as natural. I even thank it for its help. The crocodile wants to alert me to possible danger and doesn't know it is exaggerating. We are not in a life-or-death situation, even though the reptilian part of me feels that way.

Mimi not responding means something is happening that is different from what I expected. In the wild, when something unexpected happens, it can mean we are about to be attacked by a predator. Better to be safe than sorry, signals our crocodile. Get ready to be attacked!

Our reptilian brain instantly labels the source of our unmet expectations as "danger." The crocodile conjures up a frightening picture of Mimi, ensuring we stay on edge around her. Our crocodile is cunning. It works so hard to keep us alive, even if it means putting misleading labels on others as dangerous.

Paradoxically, when we give into judgment, we may start experiencing what we fear. If I give into my judgment of Mimi, for example, by becoming controlling or scolding her, chances are she will retaliate somehow. In that way, the crocodile is always right. "See, I warned you," says the crocodile, "she is out there to get you!" The crocodile doesn't realize its anxious interpretations had started the downward cycle of disconnection and distrust. The only thing Mimi has done is not respond. The rest is my crocodilian interpretation of her.

Having embraced our judgmental crocodile, we extend empathy to ourselves and the other. I like to think of it as putting a hand behind my heart and their heart.

Being human is wonderful and also a challenge. I don't know anyone who wouldn't appreciate more support and empathy in their lives. We put ourselves in the other person's shoes and extend warmth to them.

What is Mimi experiencing? Likely, she is swamped. This is the start of their fiscal year; her team is changing, and her company is in the middle of layoffs. She may have a lot on her mind. She is probably stressed. Many people feel stress these days, also heightened by the increasing instability in our external world: climate change, social inequality, racism, school shootings, wars, polarization, and the list goes on. We are challenged at a macro scale. Add the challenges each human being faces in their personal lives. Who couldn't use a bit more empathy and support?

I choose to extend Unconditional Empathy, meaning empathy no matter what. Notice the strength and connectedness that come online with being Unconditional – extending the unfailing sufficiency that we all are. We acknowledge the other and ourselves as enough and already loving, lovable, and loved. No questions asked. We simply share the love and peace we are with ourselves and the other.

This doesn't mean we become doormats. We stay truthful.

I am thinking of another client. My challenge is that he operates under what we have identified as a false sense of urgency, another favorite scare tactic of our fearful crocodile: if we don't do it now, it will be a disaster! Well, will it really?

In business, very few things are so urgent that they become disasters unless we solve them immediately. I call this delusion the "small-minded emergency trap."

This client – let's call him David – is impulsive. He will call me and say, "Hylke, we have our team together tomorrow, and I need you to be there!"

"If I can, I will do it," is my response. I have also other commitments I need to honor. "Tell me more, David, what do you really need? How can I help you with that?" I ask.

Clarity is caring. I extend Unconditional Empathy to David, letting go of judgment while also staying clear and grounded.

Vast Purposefulness: Serving the Whole

Mimi still hasn't responded, and time is ticking away. Now what? Enter the paradox of not being the center of the world and yet being part of it. I don't control what Mimi does or doesn't do. My reptilian mind wants to force a solution to get reality back in line with my expectations as quickly as possible. Then I'll feel safe again. Yet the world doesn't revolve around me. I am part of a bigger whole. I let go of my tendency to want to control and instead accept what is.

And we don't stop at acceptance. Like a tree or a flower, we still have a calling to serve. The tree is wired to grow and flourish before it dies and composts itself to feed new growth. The flower is designed to bloom. We humans are designed to express ourselves in a way that is true to who we are and what is needed. When we do, we experience inner resonance. We tend to feel disconnected and out of sync when we don't. Our inner system will let us know when it is thriving.

How do I stay connected to my calling when a client doesn't respond to my call? I ask, "what is my true purpose here?"

When I was in my twenties, I had a dream. I now see it as a vision. I saw humanity as a series of half-circles formed by humans holding hands. I saw myself standing at the edge of one of these half-circles. At that moment, I felt my job was to help orient our half-circle toward light and truth so it could be in harmony with the other half-circles.

Now, in my fifties, I see this as helping people develop connectedness with themselves, each other, and their purpose. In short, I see my purpose as developing CQ.

My calling to develop CQ doesn't end with a client assignment happening or not happening. My calling nudges me to live CQ every day, in any and all situations. Again, I ask: how can I be more truthfully present, unconditionally caring, and of service here? Maybe today, it means I will do the dishes and fold some clothes. Maybe I will listen to my husband as he tells me about his day.

Purposefulness is every day and always. My teacher's teacher, Arvis, taught Zen for three decades. When she retired from teaching, she started working in my teacher's mailroom, simply being of service.

How do we discover our calling? We don't need to go on a big, complicated quest to find it. Simply ask: how can I be of service today? What makes me come alive? What gift do I have that my community cannot afford to lose?

Contemplating these questions, we walk deeper and deeper into our truth. Sometimes, we meet a significant insight. We may realize what we are here to do differs from what we've been taught. Our work may need to become more prominent; it may also need to be smaller. What is important is that we serve something bigger than mini-me. Why? Because mini-me is a very limited perspective of what we truly are. If we believe this small idea of who we are, disconnected from the rest, we tend to make myopically egocentric choices rather than being considerate of the whole organism we are part of.

Einstein wrote a letter to a grieving father and rabbi named Robert S. Marcus, whose young son had just died of polio: "A human being is part of a whole, called by us the 'Universe,' a part limited in time and space. He experiences himself, his thoughts and feelings, as something separated from the rest – a kind of optical delusion of his consciousness. This delusion is a kind of prison for us, restricting us to our personal desires and to affection for a few people nearest us. Our task must be to free ourselves from this prison by widening our circles of compassion to embrace all living creatures and the whole of nature in its beauty."

Einstein extended his compassion through this letter of consolation. What happens when you allow yourself to embrace others – all living and seemingly not living beings – just a little more today? Where does this contemplation lead you? How can it inform what you could be in service of now?

Committing to Connectedness: Breaking a Habit

Connectedness is a choice. Disconnectedness may be a habit. Disconnectedness tends to be driven by our reactive, crocodilian, autopilot programming, which makes everything about serving a distortedly small version of me.

Why care about connectedness as a leader and as a human being? I invite you to explore that question for yourself. What is your experience when you disconnect from your truth, others, and your calling? What happens when you react as a wind vane, spun by every passing breeze?

On the other hand, what becomes possible when you commit to living more of what you truly are, connecting more deeply to others, and extending your service a bit more? Your inner music will tell you whether you are in tune with what you are, whether you are playing the instrument that you are in the way it was intended, or whether you are out of harmony.

Connected, you may feel more alive.

Imagine a world where people intentionally became more connected. Imagine the fulfillment, the harmony, and the beauty we are capable of together.

Be today what you want the world to become.

To contact Hylke:

Connect with Hylke Faber, Coach and CEO of Growth Leaders Network, and award-winning author of "Taming Your Crocodiles: Unlearn Fear & Become a True Leader," "Taming Your Crocodiles Practices," and his upcoming book "The Connectedness Quotient," and learn more about building connectedness in your leaders, team and organization at www.growthleadersnetwork.com, or on LinkedIn.

Jim Carbaugh

Jim Carbaugh is a seasoned TEDx speaker, distinguished educator, and revered coach with over four decades of experience in guiding individuals and organizations towards excellence. With a deep-rooted passion for adding value to others, Jim infuses his work with the wisdom of life experiences, sports, and nature, creating transformative experiences for his clients and audiences alike.

As a co-author and graphic novel author, Jim's storytelling prowess transcends traditional leadership narratives, offering fresh perspectives and profound insights. He is a certified member of the John Maxwell team, embodying the highest standards of leadership excellence in his practice.

In addition to his role as an educator and author, Jim is the visionary founder and CEO of All Points Leadership, a renowned firm dedicated to cultivating exceptional leaders and fostering thriving organizational cultures. Jim's innovative L.E.A.R.N. Methodology of leadership and culture development has revolutionized the way individuals and teams approach growth and transformation.

With a relentless commitment to empowering others, Jim Carbaugh continues to inspire, educate, and guide individuals and organizations worldwide on their journey towards success and fulfillment.

There is a Lesson to LEARN in Every Story
By Jim Carbaugh

It was June 30 back in 2019. My time at my current employer was coming to an end, and I found myself looking out the window of my office for the last time at the beautiful view over the cornfields into the Tuscarora Mountain. As I loaded the last box into my truck, I couldn't help but contemplate how I got to that point. Automatically, my memory jumped back to the summer of my sophomore year in college, where, in one week, I would learn the difference between knowledge and wisdom. That week would also set me on a path to spreading that wisdom to others.

Like most 19-year-olds coming off their sophomore year in college, I was feeling pretty bold and excited with all the knowledge I was gaining. But it was during that summer I had an opportunity to spend a week with a man who had lived through the Depression and honorably served his country. He only had an eighth-grade education yet went on to be an engineer, an entrepreneur, and a highly sought-after expert when it came to the antique steam engine. You see, this gentleman happened to be my grandfather, whom I affectionately call my Pap.

Pap had amassed a rather nice machine shop in his basement over the years, and in his retirement years, he restored and built antique steam engines. He also made other custom-built or small production parts for local companies and steam engine enthusiasts. It just so happened that I had a week before I started my summer job, so I thought, *why not hang out with my Pap?* I thought I could help, and he was in agreement. I can still see his face as he said to me, "Jimmy, yeah, sure. Come on down. I'm only in the shop from seven until around ten-thirty. Then I go grab lunch with your grandmother. But come on in, I've got some projects we're working on that you can give me a hand with. Who knows? You might learn something."

Well, learn I did. Throughout that week, my grandfather explained to me there were five letters, and if you were able to get a grasp on each, they would. He genuinely believed these five things could get you through life.

Listen

On Monday, I was passing through the green door to his shop, ready to work. I had always wondered what he did down there, and this was my chance to finally find out. He taught me how to use one of the machines, and I went to work drilling. He came over and asked me, "Are you listening?"

"Listening? I have been doing exactly what you told me to do," I replied.

And he said, "No. Are you listening? Are you listening to the machine? It sounds like it is struggling." Pap pointed to the machine and continued. "Have you noticed the belt on the machine has been worn down and worn out? No fault of anyone, but if you listen carefully, you will pick up on it."

So we replaced the belt, and I continued. As we finished up that day, Pap talked more about listening. He said, "You know, listening is so critical. Truly tuning in to what people are saying." He continued, "I have found that through life, the biggest mistakes and misconceptions happen when people truly aren't listening. We too often listen just to respond, not to understand what was said. Like your machine today, it really didn't sound right. You really need to concentrate and listen to what is going on in your world to fully understand what is coming your way next. And never stop listening to yourself; that voice inside needs to be heard."

Listening is more than hearing words; it's the art of actively engaging and comprehending the message conveyed. It involves not just the ears but the mind and heart as well. To become a better listener, focus on three key aspects:

1. Practice attentive presence: Maintain eye contact, eliminate distractions, and show genuine interest.
2. Cultivate empathy: Seek to understand the speaker's perspective, emotions, and intentions.
3. Embrace open-mindedness: Suspend judgment and biases, allowing for a more comprehensive grasp of the message.

Enhancing listening skills involves honing the ability to absorb, interpret, and respond thoughtfully to what's being communicated.

It's about creating an environment where individuals feel heard and understood. Mastering the art of listening isn't merely a skill; it's a profound expression of respect, empathy, and connection in every interaction.

Ethics

Tuesday came, and Pap focused on doing things right. "Standards have to be met, and some of the items you made yesterday will have to be redone," Pap explained. He then added, "You know, when I come across people who just don't sound right or sound out of character, I need to tune in better. Something's off. What am I missing? You have to have a standard, and you have to have some ethics. Can't let stuff go out the door that's not right." He made sure I was paying attention before continuing, "See, it's not what you do when people are looking. It's what you do when they're *not* looking. Some people call that integrity; I call it ethics. People know when I give them a product, it's going to be what they ordered. So we got to redo some of these."

"Alright," I said. And so we did.

Ethics embody the principles and values that guide one's behavior and decision-making, reflecting a moral compass in personal and professional conduct. It involves distinguishing between right and wrong and consistently choosing actions aligned with integrity, fairness, and responsibility towards oneself and others. Developing your ethos, or ethical foundation, involves several steps:

1. Self-reflection: Identify your core values and beliefs, considering how they influence your choices.
2. Continuous learning: Engage in ethical discussions, seek diverse perspectives, and learn from ethical dilemmas.
3. Ethical decision-making: Evaluate situations based on your values, considering the implications for all involved.
4. Accountability: Taking responsibility for your actions, acknowledging mistakes, and striving to improve.

Building an ethos requires ongoing commitment and a willingness to uphold ethical standards, fostering trust and credibility in personal and professional interactions. It's a continual journey of self-awareness and conscious choices reflecting one's moral character.

Attitude

I would be a liar if I didn't admit that when I came in the next day, I had a bit of a chip on my shoulder. It was Wednesday, and I was a little hurt thinking my Pap was going to tell me I didn't do something right again. I was definitely less communicative than I should have been. After some time, he finally looked at me and said, "What's the problem?"

I said, 'You were not nice to me."

"What?" replied Pap.

"What's the problem?" I asked, "What didn't I do right?"

He said, "Hey, you need to check your attitude. One thing I've learned is that if you've got a bad attitude, you are guaranteed to get bad results. If you have a good attitude, regardless of what happens, good or bad, you're going to find your way out of it. Your attitude is going to control how you receive stuff. Think about that."

"Yeah, you're right, Pap," I admitted after understanding what he was trying to get through to me.

Attitude represents the mental outlook and emotional disposition individuals adopt toward situations, events, and people. It is the lens through which one perceives and responds to life's circumstances, often influencing behavior and outcomes. Maintaining a positive attitude involves several key practices:

1. Fostering self-awareness: Recognizing negative thought patterns and consciously replacing them with constructive perspectives.

2. Practicing gratitude: Focus on what is going well and express appreciation for the positives.

3. Cultivating resilience: View challenges as opportunities for growth, learning, and adaptation.

4. Finding positive influences: Seek out and surround yourself with supportive relationships and environments that encourage optimism and growth.

A positive attitude isn't merely wishful thinking; it's a deliberate choice to approach life with optimism and resilience. By actively nurturing a positive mindset, individuals empower themselves to navigate difficulties with grace and enthusiasm, contributing to a more fulfilling and impactful life.

When we finished up that day, he informed me I probably wouldn't be working in the shop too much the following day because some people would be coming to pick up their products, and we would also be going out to do some deliveries for other customers.

Respect

So, on Thursday, I watched my grandfather interact with all these people from different walks of life. They talked and joked around like old friends. I also noticed how much he pointed out who I was to these people as I ran back and forth to the shop to fill orders or grab the custom parts he built. He looked at me as I was walking out and coming back, telling the customers about me. "And that's my grandson, and he's going to college," he would say. "Yeah, he's in college. He's playing football. He's going to be a biologist and a scuba diver."

That entire day was rather interesting. As we finished up, he bent over a little and said, "Hey, we got to head up and get your grandmother. I'm sure she's not happy. We're late for lunch." He paused to read my face, "You want to go to lunch with us? You're more than welcome." So, I tagged along.

As we sat there at lunch, all he could do was tell my grandmother about me, how well I had been doing, and how proud he was of me, not only because I had been helping him but also because I was respectful and communicative with all his friends and customers. And I said, "Pap, come on."

He said, "No. Remember to respect people. Remember to expect respect for the environment you're in. But here's something I want you to remember, Jim. Get to know people because you must treat them how they want to be treated. Remember that." Well, that stuck.

Respect encompasses recognizing the inherent value, dignity, and rights of individuals, regardless of differences in opinions, backgrounds, or beliefs. It involves demonstrating consideration, empathy, and honoring boundaries. To maintain respect, several practices are crucial:

1. Practicing active listening and empathy: Acknowledging others' perspectives and emotions without judgment.
2. Fostering open communication: Cultivating an environment where diverse opinions are heard and valued.
3. Honoring boundaries: Respecting personal space, beliefs, and values without imposing one's own.
4. Demonstrating kindness: Courtesy towards others, regardless of circumstances, fosters an atmosphere of mutual respect.

Maintaining respect isn't just about outward behavior; it's a commitment to understanding, tolerance, and treating others as they wish to be treated. It's the cornerstone of healthy relationships and fostering trust, collaboration, and harmony in personal and professional interactions.

No

Finally, Friday rolled around. It was the last day I would be hanging out with Pap, and frankly, I had some pretty big plans for hitting the beach when we were done. I came in pretty juiced up with that relaxation in mind and asked Pap what we had going on for the day. He said, "Well, we're just going to clean up the shop here, which is going to take a little time. Then I was hoping we could talk a little bit about the week."

I said, "Okay," and we got right to work cleaning up around the shop. I walked over to one of the big old metal lathe machines. "Pap, can I run this one?" I asked.

He said, "No."

I said, "Really?"

"Nope."

"That's disappointing," I said. We continued with the cleaning, but I kept looking over at the machine.

After a few seconds, he said, "Jimmy, I told you no earlier."

"I know," I said. "But all I want to do is run the lathe once."

"You know what's ironic, Jim? You didn't ask me any questions as to why you can't run the machine."

I said, "Well, you said no. Life has taught me that no means no."

He said, "Well, that's a shame. You know, the word 'no' isn't an ending word. It should be a beginning word for questions and inquiry. It should be a word that makes you reflect on why you got that answer in the first place." He said, "You know me. I'm really big on no excuses. And that is why sometimes getting a no is really a good thing – you'll never appreciate a yes if you don't start to understand the no. And remember, no is not an ending point. It's a launching point in a whole new direction. A no doesn't mean you can't do it. It just means you either can't do it at that exact moment or with the person who gave you the no – or both. But if it's something you really want, you have to know why you got that no." I thought that was a pretty interesting explanation.

Giving a no' requires tact, empathy, and clarity. When delivering a no, be direct yet considerate, explaining the reasons behind the decision. Offer alternatives or solutions if possible, demonstrating respect for the person's request while maintaining firmness. It's crucial to convey the message without causing undue harm or misunderstanding. Dealing with a no response involves acknowledging and accepting it gracefully, which can be done in several ways:

1. Remain composed: Take a moment to process the decision without an immediate emotional reaction.

2. Seek understanding: Politely inquire about the reasons behind the refusal, helping to clarify the situation or seek alternatives.

3. Stay positive: Use the no as an opportunity for growth or learning.

4. Maintain professionalism: Respect the decision, understanding it's not a reflection of personal worth but often a situational or contextual decision.

LEARN

Before we wrapped it up for the week, Pap said, "You know, Jimmy, I've been lucky enough to learn a lot throughout my life. Tell me a little about what you learned this week.

"Well, Pap. I'll tell you what. I gained a lot of knowledge and insight on some things, such as how to interact with people."

He said, "Jim, I handed you some wisdom. On Monday, we talked about listening correctly. On Tuesday, we talked about doing stuff the right way."

"Ethics, right?

"Yeah," he replied. "Wednesday, we talked about your attitude. Thursday was all about respect." He paused, then said, "We just got done talking about no, right?"

I nodded in confirmation.

"What'd you learn? Listening, ethics, attitude, respect, and no. If you can understand those five things, as we talked about them, and practice each of them, you'll make it through life. If you learn to listen to everything in life, you're going to be good. If you find out what your core values are, you're going to avoid making bad decisions because they won't fall within your values. You will put out very few bad products if they stay within your values. What you listen to will be controlled by your values and support the development of your ethics, which will affect your attitude. If you're positive in your attitude, you'll always hear what's being said. And if you respect what you're hearing and respect the people around you, you will learn. But your biggest learning will come from getting that no. If you dive deep into the reasons you got that no, you will learn it's all linked. You truly learn when you listen and have ethics, respect, and a positive attitude. Understanding why you received that no is how you gain wisdom, and wisdom is different from knowledge."

I said, "You know, it is Pap. I appreciate it."

Three Questions to Live By

He said, "Jimmy, there are three questions you need to ask yourself every day. When you get up, ask yourself why you're here. Every day, you have a purpose. Then you gotta ask yourself what's going to be your legacy today. That gives you direction because, at the end of the day, you're going to have a legacy, and your life is built on your legacy every day. But most of all, when you sit down at night, ask yourself what you learned today. Did you increase your listening? Did you do something with your values? Your ethics? What was your attitude like? Where did respect come into play? Did you get a no and take the time to understand why you got it? Remember, you will never appreciate a yes if you don't understand the no.

Answering those questions at the end of every day will help in retaining the lessons learned. But equally important are three questions you need to ask yourself each morning because the answers are akin to setting a compass for the day, guiding actions and decisions toward a purposeful life.

"Why am I here?" This question delves into your overarching purpose, clarifying your role in the world. It prompts reflection on personal values, passions, and aspirations, aligning daily actions with a greater sense of meaning. Understanding this purpose fuels motivation, providing direction and focus in navigating life's challenges and opportunities.

"What will be my legacy?" This question dives into the impact and contributions one wishes to leave behind. Contemplating your legacy encourages conscious choices and actions geared toward creating a positive influence, whether in relationships, careers, or communities. It emphasizes the importance of living intentionally, leaving behind a meaningful imprint that extends beyond individual existence.

"What is it you want?" This drills down to immediate desires, goals, and intentions. Answering this question allows for daily goal setting and aligning actions with short-term objectives. It facilitates clarity in decision-making, ensuring that daily tasks and endeavors correspond with personal aspirations and priorities.

Addressing these questions daily fosters introspection, aligning daily actions with broader life objectives. It cultivates a sense of purpose, fuels motivation, and ensures each step contributes meaningfully to a purpose-driven life. Regularly revisiting these queries offers a compass for navigating life's complexities, fostering a fulfilling journey toward personal growth and fulfillment.

So, as I sat there looking through the window of my truck over that same cornfield into the Tuscarora mountains, I would be looking at again more than thirty-five years later, I thought to myself:

Why am I here?

What's my legacy?

What did I learn?

I've shared this message for 40 years now, and I hope that you start asking yourself these same three questions every day.

LEARN: It's not just a word; it's what you need to do daily.

Listen: Hear what is being said before you speak up.

Ethics: Do the right thing and add value.

Attitude: Keep it positive.

Respect: Treat everyone the way they want to be treated.

No: Eliminate excuses; own it and solve it.

***

To contact Jim:

https://jimcarbaugh.com/

https://www.linkedin.com/in/carbaughjim/

https://twitter.com/Jim_Carbaugh

Inquiries/Booking-

carbaughjm@gmail.com

Or

allpointsleadership@gmail.com

Angilie Kapoor

Angilie Kapoor is a highly acclaimed leader with over 20 years of experience in healthcare, 10 of those years in management roles, and 5 years of experience as an entrepreneur. As a Conscious Leadership Coach and Empowerment Strategist, she is dedicated to helping workplace, business, and life Aspiring Leaders increase their confidence & effectiveness & amplify their impact by embarking on their unique leader transformation journeys to unleash their inner phenomenal leaders. Through her extensive background in management and leadership, she offers invaluable knowledge and insights gained from her own journey.

She is also a multi-book author; her masterpieces are must-reads for aspiring leaders who want to harness their powers within. As an inspirational speaker, her unique perspective and engaging speaking style captivate and inspire audiences to be empowered to unlock their full potential and uniquely contribute to the world.

As a TV show host, Angilie brings her powerfully resonant and electrifying energy to every episode, bringing viewers on a journey that challenges their perception, shifts their awareness, and leaves them feeling deeply empowered and inspired.

Angilie is also the founder of Oversight Global, an organization dedicated to addressing the consciousness crisis in the world one leader at a time.

Beyond Myth and Fiction: The Truth About the Hero's Journey

By Angilie Kapoor

One of the most extraordinary things I've discovered in my life journey is this hidden secret that only a few people truly and fully discover and realize. This priceless secret is both simple and complex. When you discover it for yourself – you'll initially be astonished by its simplicity as a concept, yet quickly realize that the journey of attaining it is rather complex. Notice I say complex but not impossible.

Now, what is this secret, you're likely asking yourself... Well, let me explain it like this...

I kid you not that it's exactly like any story in a book that's ever been written or any movie that has ever been made using the standard plotline of the hero's journey. From ancient myths, legends, and stories to classic novels and modern-day movie franchises.

I'm sure you know exactly what I'm talking about. It's always a tale of a primary, ordinary character who is revealed to be an unknown, hidden, legendary hero or savior with latent, powerful abilities - whose purpose and destiny is to save the world from impending doom.

This journey usually begins with the hero being required to leave their ordinary life behind - joined and guided by a mentor. Together, they embark on a journey into the unknown, experiencing various setbacks and encountering various allies and enemies. During their journey, the hero undergoes a transformation by cultivating and mastering new skills and abilities and discovering their inner strength and wisdom. Ultimately, the hero emerges victorious with newfound knowledge and understanding that they can use to benefit those around them and lead a fulfilling life.

As audiences across various cultures and generations, we have been and continue to be entirely captivated by this hero's journey concept of an ordinary person who discovers within themselves an extraordinary power that sets them apart from the rest of humanity and allows them to live an incredible life.

But what if I told you this concept is more reality than fiction? What if I told you that you are the hero of your story? That YOU indeed do have within you an extraordinary power? And YOU are capable of living a life you love?

Ultimately, these stories of the hero's journey concept reflect the human experience.

They demonstrate that we all have within us everything we need to be successful in every way; that we hold the key within us to all that we seek.

The extraordinary power we all have inside us is our true, authentic, best version of ourselves, who possesses the abilities and capabilities to accomplish anything. This extraordinary power is what I call our 'inner phenomenal leader!'

We typically perceive leaders as leading others in professional or formal capacities. But the truth is, you can only lead others as proficiently as you lead yourself. Meaning, that all of us have the capability to lead. All of us are meant to lead!

I made this life-changing discovery during my management and leadership journey in healthcare and have repeatedly observed it in working with others as a conscious leadership coach. I see this secret reiterated daily - that we all are meant to lead. We all possess the innate abilities to be leaders of ourselves and our own lives. And these abilities can be extended out to lead others if that is what we are called to do.

Achieving the embodiment of your 'inner phenomenal leader' is truly a life-changing experience for anyone who aspires to lead a fulfilling and empowered life. Doing so demands a deep understanding of yourself, self-awareness, and the ability to manage your emotions and perceptions. It requires developing and nurturing confidence and self-assurance from deeply knowing and loving yourself. When you unleash your 'inner phenomenal leader,' you'll radiate calm and peace in your demeanor, even during uncertain and challenging situations.

You'll set clear intentions, which you'll pursue with unwavering determination, knowing you can achieve anything you put your heart and mind to. You'll cultivate contentment with yourself and your endeavors, focusing on the journey rather than solely on the destination. You'll be committed to self-love and self-care, prioritizing your mental, emotional, physical, energetic, and spiritual well-being.

Unleashing your 'inner phenomenal leader' means embodying an intriguing, energetic, resonating, connecting, inspiring, and empowering presence in all you do, leading others to follow in your footsteps. Being the leader of yourself and your own life is a fulfilling and rewarding journey that enables you to tap into your full potential and lead a life you truly love.

So, there you have it. The secret. Didn't I tell you it was simple? Now, why is this a secret? I'm not sure. It's not hidden per se, but it's not advertised either, and not many people know about it, which makes it even more crucial that we get more people in on it!

Now you may be thinking, 'How can that be?!' 'If each and every one of us possesses this extraordinary power deep within us, then why are there so many people struggling in the world?'

We can openly see that most people around the world, even in the United States, one of the most developed countries on earth, struggle every day with challenges in various aspects of life, including health, work, relationships, finances, and personal development, just to name a few.

You see, that's the complex part that I mentioned earlier. The complexity of this secret is our hero's journey. The journey of transformation we must embark on is learning new skills and abilities and discovering our inner strength and wisdom. We need to learn how to harness our 'inner phenomenal leader' within us to manage and master the struggles and challenges we face in our lives and the world every day.

Don't be mistaken; once you can recognize and embody your 'inner phenomenal leader,' it doesn't mean that you cease to have struggles. The struggles of daily life will continue. The difference is that you'll know how to handle and overcome them better, quicker, more confidently, and more easily than you used to.

The key to embodying our 'inner phenomenal leader' is to work through all the junk we struggle with daily. We must learn to manage and master our struggles instead of enduring them. We must learn how to be empowered instead of continuing to be disempowered because we give our power away constantly. We must learn to be intentional and in control instead of being at the mercy of others and the world.

Our struggles and limitations are not external like we think and are often led to believe. Instead, they are internal. The root causes of our struggles are, in fact, internal, and our external struggles are symptoms of them.

Allow me to give you some examples.

One of the biggest, most common struggles people worldwide deal with is money struggles. Many of us cite external factors such as a lack of knowledge, low income, a tough job market, or a lack of opportunities as to why we experience this struggle. However, this struggle is rooted in our mindset or perspective about money. Typically, we tend to have a lack or scarcity mindset regarding money. The belief that there's never enough to go around can cause us to make poor financial decisions, overspend, undervalue our skills and abilities, and overvalue material things. Many of us have the perspective that making money is difficult when, in fact, not having money is what's truly difficult!

Another example can be found in struggling with low confidence and self-esteem. Feeling unworthy can hold us back in many areas of life, from our relationships to our careers. We tend to blame external factors such as discrimination or a lack of support, but often, it's our negative self-talk and limiting beliefs that are standing in our way.

We tend to fall into various kinds of traps throughout our lives. The trading time for money trap, where we work at soul-sucking jobs just for the paycheck because we equate success with the money we make. The identity trap, where our job title or social status determines our self-worth and value. The living for the weekend trap, where we spend our weekdays slaving away at work just to look forward to the weekends which are never long enough. The conformity trap, where we conform to societal norms and expectations, depriving us of knowing and being our true, authentic selves. And the fear of failure trap, where we are so afraid of failing that we are averse to trying anything new or pursuing our dreams.

Unfortunately, as you can see, our hero's journey is not as nicely structured or laid out as they are for the heroes in books and movies. Our transformational adventures are not neatly planned out to a 'T' to bring about our learning and mastery of our special abilities and the embodiment of our inner knowledge and wisdom. Our hero's journey tends to be complex, demanding, and messy as we work to emerge from all the junk.

Unlike books and movies, we don't typically have people such as a guide, mentor, protector, or fairy godmother searching the ends of the earth to find and save us from our mundane lives and inform us of the extraordinary power we possess.

Again, our hero's journey tends to be quite difficult, tough and messy. BUT...ONLY... as difficult, tough and as messy as you make it to be. I'll let you chew on that for a minute!

Now, quite often I get asked a particular question when I describe to people what I do as a conscious leadership coach and empowerment strategist and how I help people reach their fullest potential and uniquely contribute to the world by embarking on their transformational journey to unleash their 'inner phenomenal leader.'

People are always curious to know how I got here. How did I discover that my own 'inner phenomenal leader' even existed, let alone how I embodied it and got to where I am today, helping others to do the same?

My unintentional and unforeseen self-discovery and conscious leadership journey started shortly after my promotion into my first leadership and management role back in 2014 in Seattle, Washington, USA.

The beginning of my management and leadership career was not at all what I expected. Despite having my four-year administration-management degree, I spent months in my new role feeling frustrated, confused, and overwhelmed. This particular period was honestly the most lost and hopeless I had ever felt.

I resorted to reading tons of books and taking numerous courses, hoping things would improve and I would start to feel better and more confident and effective as a manager and leader.

I even attended several workshops and conferences that only managed to overload me with information and made me even more confused about how I should go about things. I even tried going as far as becoming certified in specific skills and seeking out and working with various experts and mentors.

Yet the solution to overcoming my feelings of being lost and hopeless, confused, overwhelmed, and frustrated still seemed to elude me no matter what I tried.

Don't get me wrong, my feverish soaking up of copious amounts of knowledge did help; it wasn't wasted. On the outside, I appeared competent and confident, successfully managed my teams, and accomplished goals. Because of this, I was promoted very quickly through the management ranks – receiving bigger teams and departments, longer job titles, and bigger offices.

But on the inside, it was quite a different story. I was suffering from all kinds of different things like imposter syndrome, low self-esteem, fear, and negative self-talk. And it was not only affecting me at work but also my health and relationships at home.

And then something happened that rocked me to my very core. The day finally came when all of my anxiety, stress, and overwhelm had built up, and I finally exploded. Without any warning whatsoever, I suddenly lost my composure - I'm talking about a huge blow up! It was during a monthly meeting with a division of my team.

I can't even begin to tell you how such an unexpected, angry emotional outburst shocked my team members and me – I had always been known for being super nice, calm, and composed. Some members of my staff left the meeting disgusted by my behavior; others left in tears from my outburst and others were openly concerned. It really was the proverbial wake-up call for me.

I suddenly realized I had to figure out how to overcome all of the struggles I was experiencing, or I would end up becoming the type of boss everyone hates having.

You can bet I got serious very quickly. I pivoted in my approach, sat down, and started to ask myself and ponder some very tough questions – who was I? What did I want? How did I get here? Where was I going from here?

I then unknowingly started a journey of self-awareness and self-discovery that eventually led me on my transformational journey to recognizing and embodying my 'inner phenomenal leader.'

I got to know myself. I started to learn about who I really and truly am. Deep reflection, introspection, and studying personal development and empowerment made me realize how much of a stranger I was to myself. I had no idea who I was, what I was capable of, or even what I truly desired. I realized how powerful truly knowing yourself can be and just how not knowing yourself can work against you (oh man, did I know that for a fact!) instead of for you if you aren't aware of the power of the mind and of self-awareness or how to harness them.

I embarked on a journey of self-awareness, consciousness, and transformation. As a result, I began to lead myself effectively and be a great leader to myself, which ultimately helped me be an effective leader to others.

Bing, bang, boom, fast forward to now, and I've got multiple management and leadership successes and recognitions under my belt AND a successful conscious leadership coaching business that's continuing to grow. Today, I enjoy the joys of having time and location freedom, setting my schedule, and traveling extensively around the globe. I also no longer feel overwhelmed or burnt out, and my life is fulfilling and richer like never before, and I know that it will only continue to get better and better.

So now that I've given you some time to chew on the idea that you have more control over your transformational journey than you think you do, let's dive deeper into that.

As I mentioned, it's unfortunate that our hero's journey is not as nicely structured or laid out as it is for the heroes in books and movies.

We don't typically have someone searching the ends of the earth to find us, save us from our mundane lives, and inform us of the inner extraordinary power we possess within us.

We don't have our transformational adventures nicely and neatly laid out with speaking lines and directions on a storyboard to master our special abilities and the embodiment of our inner knowledge and wisdom.

Or do we?...

I don't believe in coincidences. I don't believe that you randomly picked up this book or randomly turned to and started reading this particular chapter. I believe that you are here right now for a reason. Actually, I know that you are here right now for a reason.

I also know that my passion, purpose, and mission are to search for and find those who I am meant to help, who I am meant to show that they are meant to be extraordinary, that they are meant to lead phenomenally, and that they are meant for more than what they are experiencing in life right now. I know I am meant to help people embark on their transformational journeys to embody their 'inner phenomenal leaders,' reach their fullest potential, and contribute as they uniquely can to this world.

With the right components, your hero's journey can be just as smooth sailing as what we read in books and see in movies about those heroes.

Luckily, I've determined from my own experience and in my working with others that five components are needed to change, grow, and thrive successfully.

They are:

- utilizing a proven strategy & process
- acquiring the proper tools
- having the proper guidance
- being in an environment ripe for growth & success, and
- making the conscious decision to become the best version of yourself and reach your fullest potential.

I have spent the last two years taking the knowledge and insights I've gained from my journey and helping others on their journeys, as well as considering these five components I've determined are needed to achieve ultimate success.

I've used all of this to create the ultimate experience, the ultimate transformational journey for the unknown heroes who are ready to tap into the extraordinary powers they have within and emerge victorious. Emerge in leading their best, most fulfilling lives and inspire others around them to do the same.

In my new 'Meant to Lead' premiere coaching experience, you'll have all the components I've determined are needed to change, grow, and thrive successfully.

Like the heroes in books and movies, you'll have an expertly planned transformational journey proven and tested to help people tap into their extraordinary powers within and embody their 'inner phenomenal leaders.' Your transformational journey will include the hands-on acquiring of the proper tools you need to learn to master your abilities to overcome your struggles. Your experience will include the expert guidance of your own guide and mentor as well as the assistance of other ability experts and fairy godmothers and fathers. You'll be surrounded by various allies in an environment to assist you in your growth and success.

However, none of this can occur until you consciously decide to know without a shadow of a doubt that you are meant to be the hero of your own story. The conscious decision to become the best version of yourself and reach your fullest potential by embodying your 'inner phenomenal leader.'

We are now at a critical point where the next decision you make, the next step you take, will truly be life-altering. It's like that classic scene from a super popular movie where an adored leader and mentor offers the unknowing hero and savior the ultimate choice: red or blue.

You can take the blue pill, take the knowledge and insights you've just learned, and do nothing different but go back to your life just as it is, waking up every day to the same routine. Or you can choose the red pill, take this newfound knowledge and awareness, and enter a whole new world of possibilities and adventure.

That's exactly where you are now - standing at a crossroads where one path is safe and comfortable, and the other is filled with possibility and potential. The choice you make right now will determine your life experience moving forward. So, the question remains: *which path will you choose?*

***

To contact Angilie:

For details on Angilie's 'Meant to Lead' Premiere Coaching Experience, visit:

www.oversightglobal.com/coaching

To book a 'Meant to Lead' Info Session with Angilie, go to: https://calendly.com/angilie_oversightglobal/meant-to-lead-info

To learn more about Angilie, visit: https://www.oversightglobal.com

To connect with Angilie:

Instagram: https://www.instagram.com/oversightglobal1356/

Facebook: https://www.facebook.com/oversightglobal

LinkedIn: https://www.linkedin.com/company/oversight-global-llc/

YouTube: https://www.youtube.com/@oversightglobal

Author Central: https://www.amazon.com/author/angiliemkapoor

Sir James Gray Robinson, Esq.

Sir James Gray Robinson, Esq. is a third-generation trial attorney who specialized in family law and civil litigation for 27 years in his native North Carolina. Burned out, Sir James quit in 2004 and has spent the next 20 years doing extensive research and innovative training to help others facing burnout and personal crises to heal. He has taught wellness, transformation, and mindfulness internationally to thousands of private clients, businesses, and associations. He is focused on helping lawyers, professionals, entrepreneurs, employers, and parents facing stress, anxiety, addiction, depression, exhaustion, and burnout.

Sir James is a highly respected speaker, writer, TV personality, mentor, consultant, mastermind, movie producer and spiritual leader/healer who is committed to healing the planet. He possesses over 30 certifications and degrees in law, healing, and coaching, as well as hundreds of hours of post-certification training in the fields of neuroscience, neurobiology, and neuroplasticity, epigenetics, mind-body-spirit medicine, and brain/heart integration. Having experienced five (5) near-death experiences has given him a deeper connection with divinity, understanding and spiritual energy.

In recognition of his outstanding work and philanthropy, Sir James was recently knighted by the Royal Order of Constantine the Great and Saint Helen. He recently received the 2024 International Impact Book Award and the Presidential Lifetime Achievement Award from President Joe Biden.

Establishing Yourself as a Luxury Brand
By Sir James Gray Robinson, Esq.

By now, most beginning entrepreneurs are familiar with sales funnels, discounts, up sales, and package deals. They believe urgency and fear of loss marketing can generate wealth and prosperity. I have lost count of all the offers that come across my computer screen, offering a product for free just to get potential buyers into their sales funnel for future sales. The theory is that when they enter the sales funnel, you have a better chance of convincing them to buy more products later. It is a standard method of marketing and can be successful. However, it requires a lot of work and a sales approach that works. Not everyone can get great results using this method.

Sales funnels are a well-established method of creating a customer journey that ends with the customer buying something you are selling. There are five typical stages to a sales funnel. First, there must be customer awareness of what you are offering. This is usually established through social media, advertising, or webinars.

Second, there must be customer interest in your product. You must create engaging content to entice awareness and interest. This is when the customer is willing to research and decide whether your product is desirable, either because it solves a problem or is being sold at an attractive price.

Third, you must evaluate what the consumer is interested in and tailor your messaging to attract their interest. Not only do you have to assess what the customer wants, you must help the customer evaluate your product. This is calculated to help the customer decide whether to choose your product.

Fourth, by this time, you must have interacted with the customer and answered all their questions or at least given them a reason to buy your product. You give them a call to action, with clear and concise steps to take to acquire your product and, ideally, what will happen to them if they don't. Fear of loss is generally the motivating factor at this point.

Fifth is decision time. All the customers' objections and questions have been answered, and they should be ready to buy. They understand that they are getting the best product for the best price for the right reasons if the funnel has been successful.

The reason that sales funnels can fail is five-fold. First, the entrepreneur sends an indirect message to the buyer that a high-priced product given away for free or at low cost isn't worth the "estimated value". When someone puts a value of $10,000 on a product that they are giving away for free or $19.99, it raises questions in the buyer's mind about the accuracy of the valuation of the product. After all, who in their right mind would give away a product worth $10,000 for nothing, even if it is a hook to get the buyer into the sales funnel?

Second, the initial "bait and hook" offer of low-cost/high-value products is usually followed by secondary offers for add-on products at higher prices. By the time you finish buying all the parts and pieces, you spend quite a bit of money. I have seen hundreds of offers using this methodology, and I usually end up canceling/deleting the offering email.

Third, these products are usually service-oriented, so there is no way to ascertain the product's true value until you buy it and receive the service. By then, you may be disappointed in wasting your time and the affirmation of the old saying, "You get what you pay for." For those who have experienced this sales model a few dozen times, it gets to be annoying and counterproductive.

Fourth, with the discount sales model, buyers are always trying to negotiate down because they already know you are willing to lower the price to make a sale. It puts the seller at a disadvantage because the buyer has the money and the power, and the buyer knows the seller will probably sell cheaper at some point just to get the sale.

Fifth, the sales funnel isn't working. There could be problems with the content, the landing page, the call to action, or a lack of clarity on why they need the product. If the messaging about the product, the price, the call to action, or what they will lose if they don't buy is not clear and adequate, the sales funnel will collapse.

While sales funnels have been highly successful for some people, they are difficult to manage and require constant maintenance and attention. The sales process is often more important than the product, which often gets lost in the process. It is critical that the entrepreneur attracts as many leads into the sales funnel as possible. When you are selling at the lowest possible price or giving your product away, you must do mass marketing to as many people as possible. This requires that the product be as generic as possible to appeal to as many people as possible. When you limit your audience to a limited niche, you could be shooting yourself in the foot because a lower price demands higher volume sales.

In contrast, a completely different marketing approach requires a completely different mindset. For people who are trying to get people into their funnel through discounts or giveaways, you knowingly or unknowingly choose mass marketing to sell your services or products. If you are trying to upsell your customers to more expensive products or services, you may consider luxury marketing instead.

All luxury companies have one thing in common -- they cater to customers who don't care about price. They have features that create allure and mysticism that create demand and attention. The marketing mindset is the opposite of discount and giveaway marketing. This type of marketing is focused on one thing and one thing only: the mindset of the affluent and wealthy. The affluent and wealthy don't care about price; they only care about uniqueness and quality.

A luxury brand focuses on aspects of the product that may or may not be intrinsic to the quality of the product. These brands are associated with wealth, prestige, and lifestyle. They connect with national archetypes perceived as superior qualities and status. They evoke emotions involving pleasure and comfort. The consumer believes that they are purchasing something unique and rare. The marketing focuses on establishing a product that is long-lasting and high quality versus a bargain.

You must build a dream for them and show them how your product will transform their life by making them more desirable, attractive, or unique. These customers don't care about problem-solving; they pay people to solve their problems. They want to surround themselves with the best and unique, whether it is products or services. Luxury providers must create an environment that caters to their ego, not their pocketbook. Customers want an experience and a sense of connection.

Your product must evoke emotions, uniqueness, and wonder. Luxury customers value authenticity and the "wow" factor over all other considerations. It may be the association with you as the brand just as much as the product. If you have a story, use the story to sell the product. Ralph Lauren is a perfect example of this type of luxury branding. He is the iconic representation of style, and his clothing reflects that.

Luxury marketing starts with understanding the characteristics of the "upper class." What is it that people emulate, desire, and cherish? What are the external attributes of the wealthy class in your market that distinguish them from the masses? Not everyone can own a Lamborghini, but they can own the clothes, cologne, or sunglasses that Lamborghini drivers wear. If you can capture the luxury ethos of your market, you will know what to sell them.

Luxury branding is selective. You must market to those who can afford your product's total value. You also must be ready to say "no" to anyone that wants a discount. You cannot earn the respect of the wealthy if you agree to discount your price. It is a tacit admission that you do not believe your product is worth its purported value. For the affluent, it is a matter of integrity. If you genuinely believe your product is worth what you say it is worth, don't discount or give it away.

The challenge for many entrepreneurs is they must have not only the appearance of their products' excellence but also that standard throughout the customer experience. Your marketing team, customer service, and sales team must ooze excellence to justify the customer's trust and sharing their wealth. Whether your product is sold online or in bricks and mortar stores, you must know the mindset of the wealthy and what makes them feel safe and comfortable. When you charge a high price for your goods, you want to make that experience a fond memory for your customer.

There are four basic requirements for luxury marketing. First, you must trigger the customer's desires and aspirations. They must feel that your product will transform their life into something better (as opposed to problem-solving). Your product should have a story associated with it that is engaging or in sync with the customer's values and beliefs. If your product is a service, make it personalized and provide pleasure, excitement, and comfort.

Second, you must make your product unique or exclusive. People who pay a lot for a product don't want to see it flooding the market. If it is a service, you can market it by invitation only or by referral. Your product must make the customer feel unique, special, and important. The product must be high quality, rare, prestigious, aesthetically pleasing, or possess high emotional value to be expensive. You are selling a lifestyle that brings pleasure and enjoyment to your customers. I have seen individuals in Hong Kong driving a Mercedes when they live in a crowded tenement. That is truly selling something they didn't need but wanted.

Third, you must create an experience for your customers. Tell them a story about you and your product and involve them in that story. You can personalize the product or your services so they know that they are getting a one-of-a-kind product. Create unique promotional materials that elaborate on the story. Packaging, customer support, and service are critical to giving the customer that one-of-a-kind experience. Marketing must convey an artistic, ethereal, or dream-like quality to enhance the uniqueness of the product or service.

Fourth, make your brand cross-contextual by collaborating with other brands or products that enrich the customer experience; if you are selling ties, cross-market with handkerchiefs and socks. If you are selling services, consider invitation-only seminars in affluent areas to enhance the exclusiveness of your services.

Fifth, customer care is just as important as the image your product projects. You must make the customer feel special and important. They need to feel heard and appreciated. The feeling that they are important will inevitably drive the next purchase.

Marketing must be out of the box. Consider evocative imagery, foreign language, or content that focuses on the customer's self-esteem or self-imagery. Consider aligning with popular causes such as the environment, social justice, or charity. Give the customer ideals with which they can align when they purchase. Luxury items are desirable more than necessary. It is more important to emphasize what the product symbolizes over its functionality. Luxury has been defined as whatever money cannot buy.

Celebrity endorsements can also play a big role in marketing. Customers identifying with endorsers would be more inclined to pay a luxury price. Customers who want to be like the endorser would likely be more ready to purchase. This requires research to see who your target market idolizes, but if you are going for more mature customers, you would want a more mature endorser they can identify with.

There are several reasons why you should consider marketing as a luxury brand for your product rather than creating a discounted sale funnel:

1. Assuming the value of your product is there, charging a higher price creates a higher return on investment.
2. You will likely be dealing with successful and intelligent customers who will appreciate your product or service.
3. You will not have to mass market or deal with large numbers of customers to make the same amount of money that you would with luxury marketing. It is a lot easier to sell one widget for $1000 than 100 widgets for $10.
4. It is a lot more rewarding and satisfying to have a luxury brand that appeals to discriminating buyers.

For those providing services, it is important to emphasize the uniqueness of the service. The qualities and credentials of the provider elevate them above the masses and justify a luxury price. They must deliver, of course, and build a rapport with their clientele that makes the client feel special and privileged. The provider must articulate what is unique about their services and why the client can't get them anywhere else.

***

To contact James:

Tel: 904.204.6910

email: hello@jamesgrayrobinson.com

website: www.jamesgrayrobinson.com

Judy Copenbarger

Judy Copenbarger, JD, MBA, CFP® AIF® is the profoundly caring, professional money guide who counsels individuals and families on the facts and agendas of money. A best-selling author, Ms. Copenbarger has penned several books, serving as a wise thought leader and financial fiduciary savvy about all family business and money matters.

With her technical background in law, strategic financial planning, business strategy, taxation and investment management, Ms. Copenbarger brings MONEY TRUTH to your life, family and business.

As a sought-after international speaker for over thirty-five years and professional planner to families of substantial wealth, Judy understands what it takes to grow and sustain wealth, which often is created through business ventures.

Ms. Copenbarger shares the process of *creating and sustaining a business* in these pages, in her books, on social media and within her online financial mastery program. Her works consider every aspect of finance: Legal and Legacy, Taxation, Cash Flows and Cash Reserves, Insurances, Banking, Real Estate, Business Interests and Investments.

Her personal business experience includes decades of successful practices serving thousands of financially optimized families and businesses, an agricultural heritage, her organic vegetable and rare fruit farms, a history overcoming challenges, strong faith, and well-loved chickens.

Judy resides in Southern California with her husband of 39 years, Larry, who is also an estate planning attorney. Their five world-changing children also live in California.

So, You're in Business.... Now What?
By Judy Copenbarger

When that entrepreneurial spirit is alive in us, it is undeniable.

You have a great idea that you want to share with the world. You have a hobby that you can turn into real dollars. You have a way to eliminate the job that you absolutely hate from your life, once and forever. You've found a way out. You've tasted freedom.

You are in business FOR yourself!

Please be clear that there is a distinction between being in business FOR yourself and being in business BY yourself. Don't try to go it alone. If you truly want your business to succeed, become profitable, and remain sustainable, you will need help along the way. Consider that you don't yet know - what you don't know.

YOUR BUSINESS DECISION TREE

Passion vs. Purpose

Because you are the captain of your own ship, you are privileged to choose whether you are in business to fulfill your passion, or to live out your purpose. Are you creating a business filled with activity that doesn't feel like work? If so, you may be developing a business grounded in passion. A music-lover could choose a business of creating, editing or producing music in order to pursue his musical PASSION to remain creative. The same music-lover could choose a business of teaching young musicians, if his musical PURPOSE is to bring more music into the world and pass along his knowledge.

Hobby vs. Business

For starters, understand why you are doing what you are doing? Is this a hobby that enhances your quality of life? Do you wake up each day eager to get your hands back on that project, develop that idea, solve that problem, and share the news? Can you continue to enjoy your hobby, even though it costs you money, and doesn't make any? Or, do you want to take that idea, product, creation to market in exchange for money?

A young mother discovered her talent for "making fake food" as a craft. She developed her hobby into a successful global business that featured artificial realistic depictions of food items. An activity that began as a creative pastime and allowed her to make money while being home with her young children became a source of considerable income, and she would say decades later, that she's hardly ever "gone to work."

Exit Strategy

If your choice is to create a business, then create your business with the end in mind. Project the long term and imagine that your business is ending months or years down the road. Are you designing your business to be sold in the future, passed along to family, or will your inventory be sold for a profit? Perhaps you have a creative combination of these exit strategies in mind. Maybe you'll give it away after you've enjoyed income over the years.

A nice couple in their sixties from the Northwest created a successful real estate management business. They created enough wealth for a comfortable retirement. They also prepared enough for their children and grandchildren to have plenty for their education and futures. Once their legacy and financial planning were in place, they understood that they could donate a substantial portion of their sustainable business to charity for an ongoing income to the causes that they cared about. They were able to give it away and do a lot of good in the process.

How you structure your business will be determined by the exit strategy that you anticipate.

YOUR BUSINESS SUSTAINABILITY

Shore up your Business Plan

To be intentional about developing a sustainable and successful business, you need to "know your market." Who else has an idea similar to yours? Are you offering a service or product, or both? Who will use your services or purchase your products? How many businesses like this exist? Are you selling to consumers, or businesses? How many possible customers are out there?

A great way to check in – whether your business is a start-up, or if you've been in business for some time, is with any business SWOT ANALYSIS. You can find many SWOT analysis templates online.

You will be creating a current x-ray of your business, analyzing its Strengths, Weaknesses, Opportunities and Threats.

Strengths and Weaknesses are characteristics that exist in the business INTERNALLY. For example, your personal talent, gifts and skills are strengths of your company. Your passion and purpose are strengths. An example of a weakness could be that you are understaffed. There is only one of you, and you need more people to help the business grow. Strengths and Weaknesses, as internal elements, are more manageable that external elements because you have some control over the issues that exist in this portion of your analysis.

Opportunities and Threats are EXTERNAL business characteristics. During the COVID pandemic, we saw examples of external elements that were both opportunities and threats for business owners. For example, a restaurant in our community created take-out pre-prepared meals and sold bundles of household groceries and supplies when regulation would not allow them to host customers. The threat was the change in law that caused them to close their doors. The opportunity was the need that consumers had access to prepared meals, paper goods and cleaning supplies that were all in short supply at the time.

As you consider your strengths and weaknesses, opportunities, and threats of your enterprise, you will gain clarity about the state of your business. You will learn ways to more intentionally implement your business plan and take appropriate action to improve your business.

You will discover what you can do more, better and differently to take your business to the next level.

YOUR BUSINESS ORGANIZATION

Your business organization has three elements. If your business is brand new, you are likely wearing many hats, and getting things done, yourself. If your business is scaling, and in you are in a growth season, you may be considering adding people to help with some of the essential tasks.

1) Your business has an element of Operations, which include the tasks that cause the business to stay in motion. This category includes developing and creating your product, delivering your services, and distribution of the goods and services to the consumer.
2) Your business has an element of Development, which includes the marketing. This is the method which helps your ideal customers find and access what you are offering.
3) Your business has an element of Compliance, which includes adherence to regulations, licensing and permitting processes, accounting, record-keeping and taxation issues. The things you need to be and stay in business legally are included in these activities.

Common mistakes that growing businesses make, in my experience, are that they fail to acknowledge the division of labor and tasks that need to happen, they engage those who can help long after they are needed, and they hire the wrong people.

A business owner owned a profitable plumbing supply company which he built from scratch. After five years of learning the business, his son chose to enter the business and allow his father to retire. His son had learned well, and was successful in the operations of the business, but had never experienced the development, sales, marketing, compliance, and "paperwork" side of the enterprise.

He hired a friend to help. This friend was also very well-versed in the technology of the product lines, but similarly had no understanding of the accounting, licensing, sales and marketing of the business products. The company experienced a slow and painful decline, only to recover years later when the appropriate team was put in place. Their new dream team included an attorney, an accountant, and sales manager with business organization expertise.

YOUR BUSINESS STRUCTURE

When you begin to operate your small business, your normal first step is to create a Sole Proprietorship. In this business structure, you name your business, "hang out your shingle", and start operations. Your expenses come from your own pocket, and you claim your income and expenses on your personal income tax return, IRS Form 1040, on Schedule C.

Perhaps you tutor students, sell your original art, offer yard work services, or publish educational materials. You can readily keep records of your expenses and income and compile the information for your personal tax return when your business finances are relatively simple. When your business grows beyond your ability to track it and its employees, you have an indication that you may want to look into formalizing your business.

Your next step is to determine when or whether to formalize your business and give it a life of its own. This could be in the form of a partnership, a corporation or a limited liability company.

A partnership is generally a business structure utilized by professionals such as attorneys, architects, accountants and medical groups.

An LLC, or limited liability company, is an entity used to protect one or more of the members from personal liability incurred by the business. This is helpful particularly for real estate owners who seek to limit potential tortious liability of tenants. A young couple in Southern California is investing in several single-family houses and offering them for rent in the Midwest. They created an LLC to hold title to their rental homes, in order to protect the equity in their valuable personal residence, if a serious injury occurred in one of their rental properties.

LLC owners file their annual income taxes on one of three forms. The IRS Form 1040 on Schedule C, E or F is used for a Single-member LLC; Form 1065 is used for a Multiple-member LLC; and Form 1120-S is used for an LLC which is filing as an S Corporation.

When the young real estate investors formalized their business, they elected to file their LLC as an S Corporation. This election allows them to pass through all business gains and losses to their personal return. They accomplished this by filing to pay taxes as an S Corporation, using the IRS Form 8832.

A Corporation may be classified as an S Corporation or a C Corporation. The substantial distinctions between the two are the differences in the tax rates and accounting processes.

An S Corporation passes all gains and losses directly through to the personal return of the business owner. A C Corporation has a two-tier system of taxation. The first tax applies when the company determines a profit. The second tax applies when the owner takes distribution of funds from the company.

A businessman living in the South began operations in an adjacent state. Knowing that he would need operating capital for many of the years to come, he chose to incorporate as a C Corporation. He understood that his personal income tax rate was substantially higher than the corporate tax rates, and he considered that there was no state income tax in the state. This allows him to accumulate funds in the Corporation to be used for future capital projects and eliminate the immediate taxable income that an S Corporation would create.

Deductible expenses for you to consider tracking for your corporate tax returns include:

- Rents
- Compensation and Salaries
- Supplies
- Office Expenses
- Travel and Entertainment
- Advertising
- Employee Benefits
- Depreciation
- Taxes and Licenses
- Subscriptions
- Professional Fees

Licenses and Permits

Once you choose your business entity, be aware of any and all legal licensing requirements in your industry and in your jurisdiction. If you are operating a business that is involved in consumables, there may be regulatory licenses and permits that you need to maintain your compliance. You may be subject to international, federal or local rules for farming, food production, hazard materials requirements, or other policies specific to your business type. Be aware that some regulations are relevant to your operations and other regulations are relevant to the geographical location, where your business was created, is operating, or where your distribution channels take you.

After you establish your business entity and formalize your operating agreement, you will open a business bank account. In order to do this, you will need paperwork to show the bank exactly how you are set up in business. It will reveal who owns the business, what roles each officer has, how taxation will occur, and where the business is domiciled. Your operating agreement and business filing with the Secretary of State will allow you to establish an EIN (Employer Identification Number), which is required for you to fund your bank accounts.

At this point, you may want to consider adding a record-keeper to your team of subject matter experts. Who will keep track of your expenses, purchases, inventory, sales volume, payroll, sales team incentives, profit and distributions? It may be time to consider hiring a bookkeeper, a fractional CFO (Chief financial officer), HR (Human resources) or payroll manager or accountant to help you keep the business organized and keep you on track for proper payroll and tax filings.

If you are scaling and have achieved some success with business volume, profit and asset accumulation, it is time to think about protecting what you've grown. For sustainability, you want to be ready for the unexpected.

When sales are lower than expected or when costs are higher than expected, you'll need cash.

When your development is working better than expected and you need capital to keep up with demand, you'll need cash.

When you hire people to help you attain the next level before you can afford it you'll need cash.

Do yourself a favor and plan for these contingencies.

Keep some cash available in savings and consider having a business line of credit available at your local bank or credit union. You may have a group of investors in the wings to help with future projects and capital needs, and don't forget the SBA loan packages are often available for just these purposes. You'll need to maintain a good credit rating to qualify for an SBA loan, so be sure to watch your leverage ratios and payment schedules.

Insurance can help you avoid a major event that harms your business beyond repair. Depending on the nature of your business, some considerations for your business are: General Liability insurance, Tort insurance, Errors and Omissions insurance, Professional Liability insurance, Employee insurance, Casualty insurance, Life and Health insurance, Key man insurance, and specific Industry Liability insurances.

For many small business owners, marketing is the fun part. You can't wait to share with others what you have created and what you are offering to the world. You create a website, you print business cards and flyers, and you are blasting your good news all over social media. Many business owners start here, and don't progress …. But you know better now. Marketing is not enough.

Marketing alone may PUT you in business, but you need the fundamentals to KEEP you in business. It's all about sustainability.

YOUR NEXT STEPS

PASSION VS. PURPOSE

Verify your purpose for the business. ASK: Make Money or Follow Passion?

KEEP OUTCOME IN MIND

Keep your ultimate objective out front. ASK: Why Am I in Business?

GOOD BONES

Implement your proper business structure. ASK: Formal or Informal?

GREENHOUSE EFFECT

Grow while protecting your business. ASK: Is adequate protection in place?

DREAM TEAM

Create your team of subject matter professionals. ASK: Who is helping me?

NEXT LEVEL

Take your business to the next level. Remember to optimize your efforts and delegate what you can to others. In our firms, we have a mantra that has served me very well over the years.

"Judy should only do what only Judy can do."

I can carry the vision for the businesses, manage the team leaders, make major corporate decisions, communicate directly with clients.

All other tasks are delegated to our capable and passional team of professionals who keep operations, development and compliance at optimal levels.

Insert your name here:

"_____ should only do what only _____ can do."

WRAP UP

In order for you to "squeeze all the juice out of this chapter," I recommend that you:

1. Identify exactly where you are in your business development.
2. Notice what next step will take you to the next level.
3. List action items to implement in the next quarter.
4. Take action. Like Nike… JUST DO IT!

Blessings, as you achieve your next level in business.

You've got this!

Final note: As I write this I am gazing over an indescribably beautiful vista.

Each business we have created over the years began with the principles of the words on these pages, much hard work, and dedication. In some instances, many years of hard work preceded the fruits of our labor. Now, we as we enjoy business ownership, employing many who provide for their families, sharing business, financial and legacy principles that enhance lives throughout the country, we are in a good place. Be encouraged that the business fundamentals you put into place will benefit you for many years.

The view in front of me accompanies a soft and pleasant breeze. Fluffy white clouds are drifting by and kissing the towering and steep green mountain tops beyond the glistening bay and gleaming waters of Bora Bora. It's beautiful here.

***

To contact Judy:

www.JudyCopenbarger.Today

Judy Copenbarger 949.551.1116

Dona Kappmeyer

Dona Kappmeyer is a 3rd generation entrepreneur from San Antonio, Texas. After growing up and working in a small family-owned business, she spent the next three decades supporting respectable large and mid-sized corporations in the equipment, transportation, manufacturing, telecom, media, and outdoor advertising industries. The breadth of her career spans accounting, process improvement, operations, leadership, and small business ownership.

In 2022, Dona took the leap back to her roots to support small and midsize businesses as the owner of ActionCOACH of Coastal Bend (business coaching) and KAPPital Gain Plan, LLC (business process consulting). Dona believes that success happens when she guides individuals towards accomplishing their goals, once believed unachievable, and by contributing to the greater good. She does this by making sense of complex issues and ultimately brings simple and effective solutions that can be easily implemented in the business.

As a Certified Executive Business Coach, CPA, and Six Sigma Master Black Belt, she is seen as a leader, mentor, educator, and change agent. She truly understands the everyday challenges that businesses face, including communication, team engagement, management, production, delivery, growth, and execution.

Dona is married to Charles, and they have two amazing adult children, Chuck and Cymbrey. When she is not working, you will frequently find her and her family fishing in the bays or offshore in Port Aransas, TX.

When I Grow Up?
By Dona Kappmeyer

As children, we often dream about who and what we want to be when we grow up. "I'm going to be a doctor!" I'm going to be a lawyer!" I'm going to be a fireman!" It amazes me how specific individuals seem to have a clear sense of their identity and purpose from an early age, a phenomenon that I, admittedly, did not experience. For most of us, the reality is simple... we just don't know. There is a beauty about being young and able to dream big, free from any expectations except for our own, and then there is this thing called "life" that unexpectedly gets in the way. We begin to have these experiences that shape and influence us in differing ways. Our family members, schoolmates, where we live, the people we meet, and the places we travel to all start to heavily influence who and what we become. The clarity of our sense of self becomes more clouded, and our self-imposed destination changes. In our youth, we often think of our future career as a destination and something that we should know "for sure," but is it really? I am here to tell you that's not the case. Life is an iterative process, full of trial and error.

Let me back up. So, who is this, Dona, with one "n," and what does she know about this subject? Side note: If I had a nickel for every time that I was asked about the spelling of my first name, I probably could have accumulated a small fortune, but I digress!

I was born and raised on the Southeast side of San Antonio, Texas, in a family with two awesome parents and five children – four girls and one boy. I was child #4. It is interesting how order and even gender play a significant role in where life takes you. When you fall further down the line, you get to do a lot of observing, and you have the luxury of sitting back and thinking, "Do I want to go down the path of my older siblings and make those same mistakes, or do I want to create my own path and make my own mistakes?" I'll take option B for $500, Alex.

I grew up in a small family business called Service, Parts & Machine Company, aka "The Shop." The Shop was started by my grandparents in 1938. After a tragic accident in July of 1952, my grandmother was suddenly faced with the reality and the burden of running the business on her own. Did I mention that this was an automotive clutch and brake rebuilding business? Imagine back then what she went through. Female owners in that industry were scarce, and even fewer women overall were in that field. But she did it! She persevered and successfully kept the business going, with grace to boot! She was a savvy, classy businesswoman and an even more incredible grandmother. In the late 1970s, my parents "officially" assumed ownership, and as a child, I was exposed to the good and the bad of running a small business. Here are some valuable lessons I learned and the experiences that began to shape me.

The value of a strong work ethic. Arnold Schwarzenegger said, "You have to work your ass off. There is no magic pill." He also said, "No one is going to do your push-ups for you." How true is that! My mom and dad worked extremely hard, running a business while raising a big family at the same time. I often look back and wonder just how in the heck they did it all. You've heard the statement, "It takes a village," and my older sisters should take some credit for that. I am very thankful that my parents instilled that work ethic in me.

The value of customer service. My dad was the epitome of customer service. He would give the shirt off his back if someone needed it and did it with a smile. It was not uncommon for him to get a call at midnight, "Hey Johnny, we have a truck down and need a clutch." My dad would get dressed, head down to The Shop, and meet the customer, never giving it a second thought. Want to know the secret to longevity in business? Simply put, if you take care of your customers, your customers will take care of you. It's not rocket science.

The ins and outs of running a business. At around the age of 10, I got to get my hands dirty, tearing down brake shoes and clutches, getting all greasy, and then cleaning, painting, and rebuilding those same parts to make them like new. It was pure "sweat equity," as we had no AC in The Shop. As I got older, I could work the counter, selling parts directly to customers, performing the dreaded annual inventories, and then "graduating" to working in the office. Now, the office was the ONLY space in the entire building with AC! Everyone, I mean everyone, wanted to find an excuse just to come in and cool off. How fortunate I was to experience so many things in a business at an age when most hadn't even thought about starting their first job.

Looking back, you would think I must have already known who I would be when I grew up. It should have been clear, right? The Shop was going to be my future. Well, not exactly. Working in a small business, especially a family business, comes with certain challenges. Now let me say up front that I do love my family, and this is not a personal reflection but just the reality through my lens. One of the biggest challenges was having family members in the business. Oh, right out of the gate, Dona! Rip that band-aid off, why don't you! Well, it's true, and most businesses that have family members face the same challenges. There were five children and, in addition, cousins, in-laws, outlaws, and later, grandkids. The lines were often blurred or almost non-existent between the business and our personal lives. Topics of conversation at the dinner table or on the weekends were primarily about The Shop and were often not pleasant. We also faced challenges within our generation. The children represented the third generation, and according to the Small Business Administration (SBA), the success rate for the third generation is only 12% and drops to a mere 3% with the fourth. The odds of our future success in this business were clearly not in our favor.

I was nearing the time to begin college. "Hmm, who am I supposed to be when I grow up? Let's see. My grandfather was an accountant, my dad had his accounting degree, so, yes, I know! I'm going to be an accountant!" Made sense, right? Did I love accounting? No, but I was good at it and knew the value it would bring regardless of what I did in the future. After finishing college, I was working back at The Shop when my dad gave me the greatest gift ever. He told me, "Dona, you need to get out of here and go get a real job." "Well, thanks, Dad, I love you too," I thought. Looking back, it was more like, "Thank you, Dad, for making me leave!" It was time to put my big girl pants on and start living my option B. Real world here I come, absent the green visor, thank goodness.

Maybe it's just me, or maybe it's my generation, who knows, but with every company I went to work for, I went in with the intent that this one would be my "forever" company. That's the mindset we are supposed to go into every job thinking, right? Well, spoiler alert: that was not to be the case.

About five years into my accounting career, I decided to get my CPA license, and of course, it was not at an optimal time. Software conversion at work, a 2-year-old son, and a husband coaching high school sports, what was I thinking? I was so glad that I did, but even so, deep down, I felt that I was missing something. Yes, this license would help me advance my career, but "who do I really want to be?" often crossed my mind. Towards the end of 1999, I was on maternity leave with my daughter when I received a letter in the mail. My "forever" company had been sold, and headquarters was moving to Florida. I had a dilemma. Do I stay with the company and move or move on? Option B again. Next forever company, here I come.

Five years into working in the accounting department at this next company, I was approached by management about being a part of a small team that would launch a Six Sigma process improvement program. The equipment manufacturer of the products we sold was one of the first organizations to require Six Sigma representation throughout their supply chain, from supplier to distributor.

Six Sigma, what is that? I knew nothing about it, but I was intrigued. My inner desire to do something more was on fire, and I was all in! Maybe this was who I was supposed to be. All of us who were selected came from different backgrounds and would be entirely taken out of our comfort zones. If we look at Ken Blanchard's situational leadership model, I quickly went from a D1 - enthusiastic beginner, "yay, I am happy to be in this exciting new role", to a D2 - disillusioned learner, "crap, what the heck did I get myself into?" I knew that I didn't know what I didn't know. Yikes! But it was a change. It was going to be an adventure. I was learning and growing and understood how this would make a massive difference to the organization, the customers, our employees, and, yes, my career. I will say, hands down, this experience began to shape who my future self would be. And as with anything new, especially this, there were a lot of eyes on it. We had to be successful. Were we? Yes, and we did save the company quite a bit of money, created a lot of efficiencies, and improved processes. But we were also green. We took on projects that were too big and took too long. People were getting impatient, so we pivoted and changed our approach.

We learned how to scope down to get quicker wins. It was now working better! Then, 2008 came, and the economy took a dive. Like many companies, a significant chunk of our workforce was laid off, and our department was no exception. I was a bit perplexed by this. Weren't we in the business of process improvement and doing more with less and doing it better? I began to question whether the commitment or understanding from leadership was not fully there. Maybe these kinds of decisions were out of their hands. I really wasn't sure. And then, I began to question myself. Is this still who I want to be when I grow up?

Shortly after, it was time. I left this "forever" company and began understanding more about myself and my future. I learned to accept that, most likely, there would not be another forever company for me, at least not in the corporate world. Previously, I was of the mindset, "Let me just wait it out a while; they'll come around." I couldn't this time. I needed to move on, and I am grateful that I did. It's amazing to me how many people are still willing to sacrifice their happiness because of a fear of change and are OK with putting their decisions or indecisions in the hands of others. Life is too freakin' short! I decided to stop waiting for things to improve when I could not influence the situation. I looked for the next step in my journey. Now, where am I going to find fulfillment? I asked the same question, "Who do I want to be when I grow up?". Over time, it got easier to move on to other companies. I encountered both positive and challenging experiences, but I am nothing but grateful for the lessons and insights I learned along the way.

Fast-forward to the era of COVID, I was working as an executive for another company. The widespread "lockdown" impacted countless individuals; our company was no exception. We transitioned to 100% remote work within a few days and thank goodness we already had the technology at our disposal to function without a miss. Email, instant messaging, cell phones, Zoom, you name it, we were connected. Did I say THANK GOODNESS we were connected? What was I thinking? We couldn't disconnect!

Everything we did had to be planned and scheduled. Zoom meeting after Zoom meeting with some of the same key people on each call.

How did we get anything done? We were working so much harder and not getting near as much accomplished. We were genuinely living Einstein's definition of insanity, expecting different results while doing the same thing repeatedly. What was missing? That real in-person, human-to-human interaction. The ability to get out of your chair, talk to someone, and discuss the situation was gone. No more water cooler talk. Some were so excited about the convenience of working from home. And yes, I will say it was convenient. After so many years of long work commutes, it was a welcomed change, but that was short-lived. The conditions were less than ideal for a team that thrived on extensive interpersonal engagement to accomplish tasks. And, if you were a people person from a behavioral perspective, this was exceptionally tough! We needed to get back into the office, but over time, that was not to be. My instincts and thoughts were once again guiding me. Do I want to persist in a situation where I cannot perform at my best, or is it time to make a change? I'll go with option B for $500 again, Alex.

Looking for the next career opportunity during that time was not easy. After leaving, I spent the next few months doing some serious soul-searching. I was asking those same questions again. "Who do I want to be when I grow up? What am I doing with my life? What is my purpose? Was the past 30 years working for big corporations a waste?" Then, I swiftly pivoted. I pondered: How can I harness all of that experience for a purpose greater than mine? I began researching different kinds of franchises and explored the prospect of engaging in independent consulting. I hired an executive coach, Arlene Post. I began contacting individuals in those spaces, and then something happened. Lo and behold, I reconnected with an old acquaintance of mine through LinkedIn - Rory Sheppard. Rory had started a franchised business coaching firm in West Texas called ActionCOACH, and I wanted to know more! He was educating, mentoring, and coaching an underserved market of small and mid-sized business owners. That one-hour conversation with him in January 2022 changed my life. What was I waiting for? Nothing! Count me in! Within 30 days, I had my own franchise. Did I know what I was getting myself into and what my future would look like?

No, and was I OK with that? Yes! My desire to change and be a part of something bigger than me and the opportunity to help so many small and mid-sized businesses grow far outweighed my fear and my resistance. "This is who I am supposed to be when I grow up!" I thought. Now, two years into owning a franchise in the Coastal Bend region, along with a process improvement consulting firm, KAPPital Gain Plan, LLC, I haven't looked back. Has it been easy? Not at all. One of Jim Rohn's famous quotes is, "Never wish your life were easier, wish that you were better." I have never exerted more effort in my professional life, and I've never found as much enjoyment in my work as I do today. Each morning, I genuinely wake up excited – what a remarkable feeling!

I could continue with so much more, but that's a story for another time. What is the moral of all of this? Well, surprise! There's no perfect time in your life to know who you will be when you grow up. Circumstances change, and guess what? You get to decide again and again and again. The world is constantly evolving, and careers 5, 10, and 20 years down the road haven't even been invented yet. Whether perceived as right or wrong, good or bad, you are where you are precisely meant to be. Life is a journey and not a destination. I genuinely believe that life unfolds the way it is supposed to, and over the course of time, your experiences have and will continue to shape you into the person you are right now and the person you will become in the future. Listen to your instincts, pay attention to the signals you receive, and act without hesitation. Following this path will allow you to become the best version of yourself. And really, what is there to fear when the most significant risk is to not take any action at all? One final thought: Growing up is overrated. Don't do it!

***

To contact Dona:

donakappmeyer@getintoactionnow.com

http://www.donakappmeyer.com

http://www.getinactionnow.com

https://www.linkedin.com/in/donakappmeyer

Mark Yuzuik

Mark Yuzuik was raised in a family where he was one of 4 boys and one sister. He witnessed his parents struggle through many hard times and swore to himself he would find a way to become wealthy so he could take care of his family. As time passed his thirst for creating wealth turned into a passion for helping people.

Mark is an author, speaker, transformational coach and businessman. His true love of helping others succeed and has been performing since 1991 all over the world with his funny and powerful hypnosis shows. With over 10,000 shows, and over 8 million people worldwide he still says he too can find the fun and humor in preforming. Nothing beats the smile of an audience when looking out from stage, watching thousands of people forgetting their problems and enjoying the moment.

Mark touches the lives of people everywhere he goes. Mark is an avid student, surrounding himself with mentors and people that hold him accountable to the standards he needs to live by in order to maximize his talents.

Mark conducts multi-day seminars along with his partners in the areas of Real Estate Investing, business, Personal Growth, and Hypnosis. He teaches his students that simply having the knowledge is not enough…setting your mind up to take consistent actions is the key to success.

Mark's passion for making a difference shine through in his words and presence.

Can't Hypnotize Me, I'm Smart and Strong Willed. LOL, Yeah Right

By Mark Yuzuik

Can you remember a time when you did something, met someone or happened to be at an event, that your life would be forever different than you thought? Maybe it was a new opportunity or relationship you created just by showing up somewhere and a different path was born. We plan our lives as we feel would be the best decisions and turns out that one small event changed everything. That's exactly what happened to me. It was in the Fall of 1985 when I saw something at the fair in Phoenix, Arizona that would change my life forever. It was not a ride or anything I ate. It was mind blowing, unbelievable and no possible way that what I saw was real! Oh, was I wrong! There I was sitting in the audience of a hypnotist show, that's right, a hypnosis show. I am, what I would say, "an intelligent strong minded individual and not at all gullible". There was no way I was going to buy into that stuff. The hypnotist was famous all over the US and Canada. His name is Terry Stokes, and what a show he did. He is the best entertainer I've ever seen, even to this day.

So how is this story going to help YOU create more in your life? More of what you want! What if the answer was more of what YOU wanted and have strived for your entire life to achieve and just haven't been able to quite get it or master that skill (if indeed it is a skill), then this is what I'm talking about. More on how you will be able to achieve what you want is a bit further in this chapter.

After seeing what I saw and experienced, I developed a friendship with Terry and asked him if he would teach me how to become a hypnotist. He said no I won't teach you that, however you go to a school that teaches you how to hypnotize people, I will teach you how to become an entertainer using hypnosis. I asked him what was the difference? He said *"anyone can learn how to hypnotize people, however it's what do you do with someone after they are in hypnosis. Are you wanting to become an entertainer or hypnotherapist"?* I said entertainer. He told me that first, understand how the mind works and know that you are about to embark on a very powerful tool. This will allow you to entertain as well as empower people to make great changes in their lives, when used properly. I will only train you if you are ethical and moral. Your intentions, and what you pay attention to when dealing with people while using hypnosis, will be life changing for you and those you influence. Whether it's an audience of thousands or helping someone personally. That's why you MUST go to school first, then we can talk. And so I did, and he kept his word, Terry Stokes taught me how to become the best entertainer I can be. Over 10,000 shows in front of over 8 million people so far. I've traveled all over the world making people laugh as well as teaching people how to use the gift of hypnosis to make changes in peoples' behaviors. Working with so many artists and influencers has been more than a blessing. I have also had the privilege of teaching others the art of stage hypnosis as well, both in a group, as well as spending a month with me on tour and practicing daily getting experience.

Let's get right down to the point of this chapter and how it will affect you personally.

Do you know anyone that procrastinates, has fear, and has not yet reached their potential or goals? Maybe focusing on things that they don't even want to think about or focuses on the wrong things only to feel the way they don't want to feel? Does that person have any resemblance to you or look like you? LOL.

I love it when I hear the statement *"NO ONE CAN HYPNOTIZE ME. I TOO SMART AND STRONG WILLED, HYPNOSIS IS FOR WEAK MINDED PEOPLE"*

Are you thinking the same thing? Are you now or have you procrastinated in the past? Have you ever been influenced by fear before? Why is that? Why would you or anyone for that matter have a mission, goal or desire to succeed, get the knowledge, information, and even get excited only to let that slip away? Or put it off until the "time is right"? "I can't be hypnotized "and yet you still comply and do things you don't want to do (like procrastinating and have fear). I want to give you my definition of what "hypnosis" really is, and then you tell me if you have ever been hypnotized. Or maybe you are being hypnotized and don't even realize it. "Oh no, not me, I too strong willed". Yeah…ok…

Hypnosis: someone says something to you, you see, feel, hear or experience something and believe it to be true and then react to it... It is nothing more than a program on our minds that we received from a past event or experience that we are responding to today. Think of it like this. Imagine your computer, and the hard drive on that computer; is it possible that you could pick up a program, or virus on your computer that is not allowing you to receive the best results you want, without you even noticing that you have a small virus or program? That is possible, right? Well, what would happen if you didn't fix that problem or even worse just pretended that your computer is just fine the way it is? Does that make the problem go away? No, it does not. Not only that, guess what else will happen? It will continue down the road and will proceed to pick up even more viruses without you knowing it. However, before long, BOOM, you notice that your computer is not responding as you need it to. Right? You need a different program on your computer to clean out your hard drive. Are you getting the picture? Sounds familiar? Do you see what I am saying? So, ask yourself "is it possible that you could have some programs on your mind that are not giving you the results you currently want? Is it possible that you or someone you know is focusing on things they don't want to focus on to feel a way they don't want to feel, and they do it anyway? Why is that??? Is it really that easy to be influenced? Is all this really a story that other people want you to believe? Is this reality or an illusion? What do you think? Isn't reality nothing more than your story or even someone else's story, that you start to believe? Maybe you yourself have created a story and believe it, and because you believe it your actions will confirm that the story is the truth, and that now becomes your truth. But if all stories can be created from an illusion and all illusions become reality for us, then can't we create our own story?

What if you forgot the story you've been telling yourself and you had an opportunity to create a new story, what would that be? What if you created a story that became reality, where would you be in life? Imagine that your entire life is a story that you tell yourself of what is real and what is not. Do you know that your mind does not know the difference between reality and imagination? That is true. Have you ever imagined that you wanted something, and you got it? You didn't know how it was going to happen, but you were absolutely convinced that it was in fact going to happen and it just did. Hmmm, interesting. Or someone was going to call you and they did? Just as they called you, you probably said, "I was just thinking about you," right? Is that just a coincidence or what? Whatever you think it was, you're right. It's like a movie, that's how powerful your mind is. So that being the case, why don't you start now, creating your own illusion (reality) and stop living in other people's movie that you really don't even want to be in, let alone be the star in it? This thing called life has many chapters and sequels to it. Here is where it becomes immensely powerful! You are now the writer, director, creator and editor of this movie. How do you want it to be? Who do you want in our new life (movie) and who do you cut out of it? Maybe now is the time to get new people in your life so your movie (and your mind) is exactly what you decide it to be! Imagine right now you are in full control of everything, everything you ever wanted to do, have and be? What does that look like now? What books are you reading? What events are you attending? Who is your new influencer of peers, mentors and friends? Listen to people that want more for you and that invite you into their circle of true friends and peers so you will be *creating the life you want*. (That is also the name of my book, you can receive it as a gift for reading this chapter. Just go to my website at www.successcombination.com).

As you can see by now being "strong minded" or stubborn as I like to say, will only prevent you from having an open mind. Being open-minded is what offers you the opportunity to have the life and lifestyle you were unable to create for yourself before. The power of "hypnosis" is all about being influenced to have an open mind, so you do attract and control the things you want in life. It's not about losing control but being in control of the right programs you respond to. Are you now open to taking control of our life and creating a new program that will allow you to attract the things in life that you always wanted and knew you deserved? Knowing what is going on in your mind and who you allow to influence you is what takes you to the next step. This is not only possible but very do-able. Just because someone tells you *"You can't do that"* or *"that's not possible."* That is THEIR belief and story, not yours. That is only their limitations of what they cannot do and will never achieve. Trust me, some people will try to lower your abilities and beliefs, so they don't have to raise their own. If you only knew how many people, I got a "divorce" from in order for me to achieve more, you would be surprised or maybe not. You can still have them as friends and family, just not as influencers. Remember this, no one can influence you unless you allow them to. No one can. If you start to believe *"their limitation"* then that now becomes your limitation too. Rewrite the story where you become the leader and let them catch up.

"But what if I can't stop thinking about my past and "I'm not getting ahead"? Do you feel stuck at times, and you really are trying, and you just keep hitting a wall? I get it. I remember one time when I was studying for my Total Transformation event I was doing (3-day event) and as so many of the mentors I learn from, my wife Yolanda Martinez, who is a powerful coach for women with her *21 days with Yolanda* program (**www.21DaysWithYolanda.com**). Yolanda is writing her own chapter for the next book. Jim Britt, Michael Stevenson, Michael Nitti, Bob Proctor, Chase Hughes, Michael Silvers, Mamie Lamley, Tony Robbins and so many more than this stuck with me. It was Tony Robbins that said:

"Your limitations are not based on what you can achieve, it's based on what you feel you deserve. Society will also convince you that it's not your fault and allow events to create your meanings and limitations in life, instead of looking for the empowering messages from your past. Everything you have in life is based on what you feel you deserve not what you can accomplish".

Wow. I started thinking about why people are still stuck and have pain; maybe, just maybe, people tend to focus on what they are not getting instead of how they can give back. We cannot change events, I get that, however that one thing we are in control of is what things and events mean to us. That is how we get rid of the pain. We are in control of what we say to ourselves, not anyone else. We are also in control of what things mean to us. Never allow anyone to try to convince you otherwise. Ask yourself this: Who is in charge of your mind? You are, right? Who is in charge of what we say to ourselves? Once again, you are! Unless we give that power to someone or a past event that is not happening currently. Right? Why we still have pain in our life is simply that we are focused on what we are not getting, instead of what we are not giving. This is our mind being in survival. The pain is there because we haven't got the lesson. How you take events, and never ever give the power to someone or something else, is to look for, and find the empowering meaning in it. I am not saying that what happened in the past is ok at all, it is not. What is not ok is to still allow the past to keep influencing us in a negative way.

Why is it that some people that are given everything and have the "perfect upbringing", financially successful parents, that seem to buy them everything they want, the best college, cars for their high school graduations or birthday, or whatever they want they get…etc. They really do not have anything to worry about, some seem to have more problems than others. I am not saying that everyone is like that, some grow up and do make a huge difference in other lives as well. Let's also face the fact that some may have alcohol abuse and addictions, drug problems, cheating, workaholics or whatever that "distraction" is for them. They had it all, so we thought. And yet on the other hand we have those that have been abused mentally, physically, spiritually, sexually and other ways of being violated.

However, some of them grow up to become super achievers in life too. That is because we say, *"Never again will I ever let anyone or anything take my mind, body, freedom or life from me again, never".* The difference is that we took our pain and found a way to channel it, so we help others avoid that same pain we had endured. I'm not saying that the events that happened were good in any way, what I am saying is that when you find a way to look for the empowering meaning in that event, and that situation, you take your power back and no one will ever control your mind again, ever. Look at some of the super achievers out there and what they did. Oprah, Tony Robbins, Nelson Mandela and now, even you, that's if you decide that's the way it is. Not someone else, you! Remember this, our brains are designed for one thing, "Survival", that is just the way it is. So, when we see, hear, feel or experience something that sticks in our mind we will react to it. Now here is the difference, you decide what story you are going to tell yourself and how you are part of the solution, and by helping others that may have gone through what you may have experienced in the past.

The reason that people still have pain from their past, is because they have not got the lesson. The lesson will empower you and others to have a very compelling future and be in control of the way you want to feel and create the actions you desire to take.

In my 3-day Total Transformation event we will teach you even more on how to change the story and create an impelling future. Plus, I will teach you how to hypnotize others as well. That is so much fun seeing everyone learning this skill properly.

I remember one event in particular where we had this young girl (Morgan) just 13 years old, during one of the sessions we have people break through a board, we do this as a metaphor that when you follow through in life, you get the results you want. Sometimes doing some things in life are a lot easier than you imagined. Have you had that experience before? Remember, our imagination can work for us or can create an illusion that something is not possible. I remember that my wife, Yolanda was working with Morgan, who was very shy when she began the event, had realized by the 2nd day, she was the one inspiring others, and when she broke through the board she just started crying with joy. You should have seen her parents, they cried even more. I share this short memory because of two reasons. First, Morgan is an immensely powerful young lady today and is no longer shy. More importantly, her mom Michelle Quinn became a motivational speaker and is also in this book with her chapter. If it were not for Yolanda, mentoring Morgan and Morgan deciding that she really wanted more in life, where would her mom be? When you think that you don't have anything to share because no one is watching you, you are wrong. You are an influence on more people than you ever thought and by pretending you're not, you are just lying to yourself and hurting those that love you and who really need YOU NOW!!! Now is the time to take your life back and make some differences in other people's lives as well. Pay it forward, empower others and yourself, YOU deserve it.

Get my "Love & Wealth" program (8 audios & 2 PDF workbooks) for reading this chapter for only $47.00! This is over 90% off ($597.00 value). Go to www.successcombination.com and put in the code "family" and I will also have you and a guest at my Total

Transformation live event ($997.00 value). See you at our next event!

***

To contact Mark:

https://www.facebook.com/Hypnotistmark

https://youtube.com/c/MarkYuzuik

https://www.linkedin.com/in/markyuzuik

https://www.instagram.com/markyuzuik/

Markiesha E. Wilson

Management consultant, leadership coach, speaker, and author Markiesha Wilson equips and encourages professionals to lead their teams authentically and pursue joy in their careers.

As a coach and speaker, Markiesha ignites growth through challenge. She provides essential insights to help emerging, mid-level, and senior leaders navigate their careers from recruitment to retirement. Markiesha guides leaders to discover and refine a productive leadership style, creating fulfilling work environments for their employees.

In her book, *In the Climb: Eight Audacious Actions to Overcome Life and Climb the Corporate Ladder with Joy*, Markiesha outlines techniques to strategically navigate necessary nonsense in the workplace, excel in leadership roles at Fortune 500 companies, and heal from personal challenges.

A human capital professional, Markiesha has more than 20 years of proven experience in strategizing and partnering with leaders to design and empower dynamic workforces. She skillfully provides the tools and change management plans needed to navigate delicate, complex organizational changes and communications challenges impeding business goals.

Markiesha's successful career resume includes leadership roles with companies such as Booz Allen Hamilton, Fannie Mae, First Bank Virgin Islands, Accenture, and Deloitte Consulting. She received her Master of Arts degree in Human and Intercultural Communications at Howard University and her Leadership Coaching Certification at Georgetown University. She is certified by the International Coaching Federation.

Give more. The Surprising Answer to Life's Big Questions

By Markiesha E. Wilson

What are you doing here? I mean, what are you really supposed to be *doing* here?

All education systems fail us. No matter what part of the world or how well it's funded, every school sets us up for failure for one main reason. Our schooling teaches us that if we have a question, we will get an answer simply by raising our hand. Life doesn't work that way at all.

We asked our parents why and how I was born. We ask God what is my purpose? We spend our lives asking questions, and some never get answered. My life, and maybe yours, has been lived in phases of questions. When I was very young, I asked, "Who am I?" I yearned to know who I belonged to because love wasn't flowing from my parents like my 5 through 15-year-old self-expected and needed.

You see, my earliest childhood memory isn't pleasant. I remember walking up the street with my brother and sister, carrying my favorite pillow on a dark and chilly autumn night. I don't know much except that my mother sent us to my grandmother's, about six houses away. The streetlights looked blurry because I was crying so hard. I asked why we had to leave Mom.

Then I asked who I was in my teens and college years, wondering if I was too black in some circles and not black enough in others, too smart in some circles and not smart enough in others. As I entered corporations, I struggled to figure out how much I had to assimilate to survive or excel. Daily, I questioned, who am I really?

Suddenly becoming a single parent of my late sister's daughter led me to spend days, weeks, months, and years asking, why me? Once I found success at the top of the career ladder and raised a well-educated, self-reflective, creative, ambitious, and strong young black woman, I began asking who I am now.

If we are honest, I think we spend a lot of time asking questions, raising our hands, and getting no answers. Am I good enough?

Should I stay in this job? What do people think about me? Will I ever achieve my goals? Why am I alone? Who will love me? Do I love myself? Does anyone see me? These are questions with no answers. I've lived a life riddled with these questions.

Digging deep, we can excavate the fundamental questions that need to be answered, like what's missing and what I need to focus on. If we remain curious about ourselves and others, we stay in a learner's mindset and avoid a judger's posture. I believe our minds are sometimes better left wondering instead of googling for absolute answers.

So, who are you? What on earth are you supposed to be doing? Lately, we've begun to believe that all humans have superpowers, right? People are claiming every superpower from empathy to telepathy.

Don't get me wrong, I love the idea of having a superpower. I'd choose to be invisible. I think I'd be able to get around faster and learn what people say and do when they think they're alone. Being invisible would be the best way to observe my clients.

Knowing your *purpose power* is far more critical. What are you doing here? I mean, what are you really supposed to be *doing* here?

What is your purpose power? How do you find out if you don't know your purpose? If you raise your hand, this is a question I can help answer. When you take a self-inventory and identify that thing, service, talent, or expertise that you love to give away, that is where you find your purpose.

What is something you love and are naturally gifted to do, and would you give that for free? I believe you discover what you are meant to do through the purpose power of generosity. In your own little universe, your community, your home, your workplace, your school, your family, and your life, generosity is genuinely about living out your purpose. Generosity is my purpose power. You can change your world when you wield generosity as your purpose power, too.

Many believe you must be rich to be generous as if money is the currency of generosity. This limited thinking is one of the reasons that selfishness abounds worldwide. It's easy to think this because when we hear about large-scale generosity, it is often tied to a multibillion-dollar company. Unfortunately, many companies only give to causes to improve their image enough to sell products to certain communities, not out of true altruism. I agree with Simon Sinek, who said in an interview on the YouTube channel *Capture Your Flag* that true generosity must not be transactional, for generosity is the sacrificial act of extending oneself for the good of the other without expecting anything back (Sinek, 2014).

Generosity is an abundance mindset that doesn't have anything to do with financial stability or wealth. It's time to ask ourselves why we don't give more. Do we fear giving somehow means we won't have enough for ourselves? Are we hung up on what people do with what we give them? Worse yet, do we refuse to give because someone may become better than us?

We are generous when we see a need and seek to meet it. If we see a coworker needing help and our first reaction is; I can't give this information because it may give them more power, we are not being generous.

What is possible in our relationships when we exercise generosity? What if we give time, advice, and knowledge to the next generation of leaders in the workplace without fearing competition? Or if we offer workplace wisdom to our team members without criticism. I have spent my life giving my knowledge, time, money, and encouragement. And I want to give more of these as long as possible. I give because I remember what it was like not having, and I don't want others to feel that way.

Growing up with my brother and sister, my mom worked two jobs to care for us. She insisted we live in apartment complexes in the nicest neighborhoods to attend the best schools. One day, my mother didn't have money to buy groceries.

"Ask your father for money for hotdogs," she told me. "He rarely pays child support and right now we need it."

He responded, "She shouldn't have moved you into that expensive neighborhood."

That statement fueled my desire to become and remain financially independent throughout my life.

The joy I feel when I have given someone something they need affirms that I'm operating in my purpose power. Have you felt this joy? Sometimes, something gets in the way. Often, we are the something that gets in our way.

R&B singer Erykah Badu sings a song titled *Bag Lady*. Her lyrics describe how the bags we carry eventually get in our way. At 21, I entered corporate America as Assistant Director of Admissions at my alma mater. I had just graduated, and now I was responsible for admitting students. The first in my family to graduate with a college degree, I worked in a job with a big title and an assistant. I worked to increase the number of minorities in the university. It was important to me to be generous. I saw myself in other black kids and waived admissions fees.

I was proud of myself and my job but didn't feel whole. Looking back, I realize this is where I started stuffing parts of Markiesha into different bags. I stuffed them, dragged them, and hid them. A Sesame Street backpack full of childhood trauma, a Michael Jackson backpack full of preteen feelings of rejection because no boys liked me, and now I carried my Jansport from college packed tight with insecurities I was unwilling to acknowledge. Insecure because my college years highlighted that I didn't come from a family as rich in resources or love. Insecure because I still didn't have a boyfriend.

My early career days were tough partly because of the environments I chose to work in and my life outside of work. I was one of the few brown people in any office, often feeling misunderstood and unheard. I moved up to toting a Coach bag full of fear of failure. For two decades of my career, I stuffed and dragged and hid my collection of bags.

So, my dual-operating model was now well established. As a kid, I was in pain at home but in joy in school. As a young professional, I was tasking everyone and masking myself. I asked why wasn't there anyone who wanted to help me?

The day had come when my bags were getting in my way.

The years and my career progressed. Success came easy, and I figured out how to navigate strategically with my skills, wit, and humor. I was quickly promoted to management in every prestigious consulting firm I joined.

In each position, I insisted on being an open leader. I shared everything I knew and created opportunities for my team to maximize their strengths and minimize their weaknesses. The weight of Sesame Street, Michael Jackson, and Jansport were barely noticeable anymore. I had gotten used to being *in the climb* with all that extra weight.

Then, I decided that if I were to get to Chanel's bag-carrying level, I would need to work for myself. So, with all my bags neatly tucked behind me, I started Wilson Chapman & Associates. Feeling confident, secure, and accomplished, I wrote about the experience. *In The Climb, Eight Audacious Acts to Overcome Life and Climb the Corporate Ladder With Joy*, the rest is Herstory.

At the end of the story, you are looking at a woman over 21 years old who achieved a few Instagram-worthy posts. However, I learned in my college days that light and darkness can coexist.

Somehow, I knew I would go to college even though no one else in my family had earned a degree. Perhaps it was my first on-campus experience when I was six years old, and my aunt took me to Penn State, where her friends called me cute and fed me hot crinkle french fries with lots of Heinz ketchup. Or was it the college book covers (remember those?) my mother bought every year to cover our textbooks? Either way, by the time I got to high school, I was sure my next step was college.

I had dreamed of attending Howard University (I had one of those book covers) but didn't get to go until graduate school. Since I grew up near Philly, I thought I'd go to Temple after high school. When my mother and I moved to Maryland, I didn't know where to go, but when the admissions counselor showed up at my school and waived my application fee, Towson State University was the answer.

From day one, I felt less than everyone else on campus. I was moved in by my mom and her best friend, Christine, because my mom didn't have a car at the time. It seemed that everyone else had two parents and vehicles of their own. My clothes definitely weren't as stylish as the others. But once again, in the classroom, I shined bright. I had a few academic challenges and graduated in 3.5 years with honors without taking a summer course or missing a party on the East Coast.

While I excelled academically and internally, I grappled with many questions. Who was I, apart from my mother? I had only been the daughter of a controlling parent, never my own person. What did it mean to be black? I had only ever had a couple of black friends. How do I date? I had only had one boyfriend, who I think broke up with me, but I'm still waiting for him to call me back to confirm.

In the classroom, I learned at the speed of light but lived in darkness outside the school. Looking back at my 17 through 21-year-old multiple selves, I see an insecure black girl striving for independence, hyper-focused on learning something about everything and nothing about herself. I thought I was free because I no longer lived at home, but I wasn't free at all. Those questions I packed in my college trunk stayed packed and remained unanswered for another decade.

So, what do we do when we are living with unanswered questions and undeserved stress? When darkness is fighting to overtake the light, and it looks like darkness is winning? For me, that's when your purpose power becomes evident. You see, what you are willing to give at your lowest point is another indication of your purposed power. It is when you find out who you really are.

While preparing to deliver my TEDX Talk in Johannesburg on forgiveness in the workplace, I worked with Thabolwethu Tema Maphosa, a young, gifted Zimbabwean psychology scholar studying in South Africa. He introduced me to the concept of totems. He explained these are your family principles; they explain who you really are. I believe it's in my moments of trial that these became clear.

Here are the totems of Markiesha Elane Wilson:

I descend from those whose hearts are like an oasis.

I come from those whose *being* is a service to their immediate and extended community.

I descend from those who make space for the people they meet and the strangers they see,

Those with tender hearts and hands that carry fragile humans in their cusp.

I am of those who love and hold dear distant elsewheres with souls anchored in courage.

I am one of those who are drawn to water,

Water as a place, water as a place of remembering and nostalgia, water as a place for grieving our ancestors who were lost,

Water as motion that beckons us to continue moving and persevering in the midst of life's tumultuousness,

Water as a place of letting go, being, and generosity.

I descend from those to whom humor is the sustaining force of their lives,

Those who laugh at despair as a way of healing.

I am of a courageous bloodline of black women who confidently assert themselves and leave an indelible mark on the sands of time,

I am Markiesha E. Wilson, the daughter of Laraine, the daughter of Layruth, the daughter of Elizabeth, and the descendant of African slaves.

I wish I had known then what I know now: that I have a purposed power of generosity.

If I could drop back in time, I would tell three-year-old Markiesha to endure negativity when you go through family drama and trauma.

13-year-old Markiesha to exemplify tenacity whenever you feel ill-equipped for the assignments in front of you.

To the 23-year-old, envision possibilities because, though you don't know where you're going, you'll have to think big to get there.

To the 33-year-old, I say embody audacity when it feels like people don't take you seriously or treat you as if you are worthy enough to occupy the spaces you're in.

To the 43-year-old, I say exhibit generosity. Give everything you have to help someone get where they want and need to be.

To my 53-year-old to 103-year-old self, I say engrave humanity.

Speaking with a young man about success, I explained that I consider myself rich because I can work where I want and when I want.

He contemplated my definition and added, "If you can and have left a framework for others to follow, then you are successful and rich."

I am proud that I left a framework in my book, *In the Climb*, where I outlined eight audacious actions to overcome and climb through life with joy.

Reflecting on this, I see those who achieved their success pouring into me and never stopping. Having reached the measure of success that brings me joy, I now owe someone somewhere, something that brings them to their definition of richness. I owe another short black girl my compliments, a young professional woman my advice, a single mother my encouragement, and fathers a beautiful example of what their daughters can become.

When I transition from time into eternity, I don't need a tombstone engraved with two dates and a limited number of words to attempt to explain who I am. Please, God, let my impact on humanity speak for me. Fifty years from now, when someone asks who was Markiesha E. Wilson, the answer is that she was a Christian black woman who inspired everyone and gave everything she could.

***

To contact Markiesha:

Email: mwilson@wilsonchapman.com

Website: markieshawilson.com.

Ryan Lombardo

Ryan Lombardo is the Founder and Director of The Longevity Exchange, a concierge functional medicine practice focused on weight loss, hormones, nutrition, and gut health.

In private practice for over 20 years, Dr. Ryan has a rare combination of Eastern & Western training in health preservation and longevity. He is one of the few nationally board-certified Diplomats in Acupuncture who is also board-certified in Anti-Aging Medicine by the American Academy of Anti-Aging Health Practitioners and Integrative Medicine by the American Association of Integrative Medicine.

He holds a Bachelor of Arts in Psychology and a Certificate of Business from the University of Wisconsin-Madison, a Bachelor of Science in Nutrition and a Master's and Doctorate of Acupuncture & Oriental Medicine from the Midwest College of Oriental Medicine, and a certification in The Science of Well-Being from Yale University. While earning his Doctorate, he created the curriculum for Nutraceutical Science and Chinese Medicine.

He has been featured in Modern Luxury's NS & CS Magazines, Self, American Spa, Day Spa, Natural Awakenings, Today's Chicago Woman, the Chicago Sun-Times, WGN, CBS News, and various other local and national media.

Follow Ryan on social media and contact him through The Longevity Exchange details below.

Ryan Lombardo, DAOM, ABAAHP, BCIM

Doctor of Acupuncture & Oriental Medicine

Board Certified Anti-Aging Health Practitioner

Board Certified Integrative Medicine

Cracking the Rich Code: The Power of Health Optimization

By Ryan Lombardo

The Concept of Richness

Throughout history, humans have pursued various forms of wealth, ranging from financial prosperity to spiritual fulfillment and enlightenment. Although most people focus on the financial arena when considering the concept of wealth, our overall yearning for richness manifests in various dimensions, including aspects such as emotional satisfaction, mental acuity, relationships, spiritual harmony, and physical health. These dimensions are interconnected and create a complete picture of our overall well-being. Perhaps the most often overlooked and underestimated aspect of richness is the richness of health.

In childhood, we value time and attention from our parents, siblings, friends, and teachers. We feel fulfilled, encouraged, and loved when we receive either or both. Sometime in our youth, we start to identify a different kind of value, specifically, financial abundance... New shoes, fancy cars, big houses, and extravagant vacations. Then, in adolescence, we notice physical attributes: tall, short, handsome, pretty, athletic, etc. As adults, we strive to learn more, establish careers, raise families, travel, expand our networks, and so on. All of this is done in the vein of achievement to support ourselves and to compete with those around us.

In this chapter, we delve into the profound connection between health optimization and the enrichment of life. Before we do, I will share my personal motivation for health and wellness riches. My dad passed away last year, and I find myself thinking about his life and how it impacted my own. As an integrative functional medicine physician for over 20 years, I have explored the realms of family history, chronic disease, aging, motivation, and well-being, guiding myself and my patients toward a state of vitality beyond just being free from illness.

I was raised in the north shore suburbs of Chicago, a very competitive and affluent area bursting with new and old money. My mom left her teaching career early on to raise their five children. Years flew by as we grew up in the 70's, 80's, and 90's; while our dad grew a privately owned parking company as a chief executive. We lived an abundant life thanks to his dedication to work and the family that owned the company. I guess we were considered "rich" for having a big house, multiple cars, etc. Comparatively, financially, we had barely a fraction of the wealth of many of the families surrounding us. Thankfully, we had plenty; and our family and friendships were overflowing with love, respect, and kindness.

From an outsider's perspective, achieving financial independence, having family and friends, and a rewarding professional life may be viewed as "having it all" compared to others less fortunate. From other perspectives, a family and an established profession may appear to be limiting factors in dreams of travel and more spontaneous lifestyles.

The constant variable for any or all of this to be enjoyable, however, is health. Truly feeling rich is to enjoy the value we have created. When our dad was in his late forties, a health scare shifted his perspective. The stress of the job and lifestyle presented the early stages of metabolic syndrome and heart disease. He had worked so hard for so long but forgot to take the time to enjoy it. A few years later, he would announce his retirement and be rewarded with a watch, while the owner sold the company our father grew for almost 200 million dollars.

The initial shock and disappointment of receiving such a small token left him pondering his legacy. He had spent the majority of his children's lives at the office, on planes, in business meetings, and in hotels with hopes of creating a solid foundation and future for his family, only to learn that his time was already paid for in the eyes of the owner; and nothing more was deserved. In response, my father chose a new way of life.

He moved around the country to be close with his children, grandchildren, friends, and family. My parents moved to Montana, Arizona, and back to Chicagoland on their quest for health and happiness. My dad had a small business passion-project and consulted for start-ups in biotech, jewelry, and media. He ate healthier, lost weight, spent time in nature, helped raise his grandchildren, and assisted in a Montessori school. Then, in an instant, illness struck again at the young age of 75; acute myeloid leukemia (an unwelcome gift from serving in the U.S. Navy roughly fifty years earlier) took him in just seven weeks. No amount of money could have saved him, and no amount of money can replace him. The richness is in our memories of him and the lessons learned from his life and teachings.

I have spent my whole professional life considering how to optimize health and prevent disease. Even as a teenager, I was frequently found at the gym and in health food stores asking questions about protein powders and supplements to help improve physical performance. Then, as I watched my dad go through various stages of health and disease, I took my first job with a biotech startup in cardiometabolic disease management. It was then that I discovered my passion for longevity medicine and pursued further education. The following sections are the pillars of my functional medicine practice.

Fueling Richness Through Nutrition

Nutrition plays a crucial role in optimizing health. Providing the body with nourishing and rich foods is essential to achieve vitality and energy. With the current data and media attention, it still amazes me that so many people continue to make poor dietary decisions. This is likely due to the increased stress and time constraints of modern daily life and the continual need for convenient on-the-go meal options. Non-nutritive processed foods are consistently marketed to us as viable meal replacements and are readily available at every grocery store, airport, and gas station alike. These so-called foods are generally made up of starches, emulsifiers, flavorings, and preservatives to help us feel full and satiated – and coming back for more. Eating this way actually depletes our energy because these foods lack micronutrients and create chronic metabolic deficiencies, which, in turn, frequently cause more food cravings and other uncomfortable physical and psychological symptoms.

Embracing eating habits that benefit your physical health also enhances mental clarity and emotional well-being. The gut-brain axis is the pathway that controls neurotransmitter uptake into the brain. Adequate nutrition provides the components for neurotransmitter production, which helps regulate brain function and stabilize mood. By feeding your body nourishing foods you establish a base for peak performance of physical *and* mental health.

Studies consistently stress the significance of a well-rounded diet in supporting health and preventing illnesses. For instance, a comprehensive review in The American Journal of Clinical Nutrition points out the link between following a Mediterranean-style diet rich in fruits, vegetables, whole grains, and healthy fats with a significantly decreased risk of heart disease and mortality (Estruch et al., 2018).

Personalized nutrition is the cornerstone of my practice. Comprehensive laboratory testing can identify deficiencies and metabolic imbalances that negatively impact health. For example, testing for micronutrient levels can help identify deficiencies in vitamins, minerals, amino acids, metabolites, and more, guiding the use of supplements and customized dietary plans to improve one's health profile. We can also test for chronic food sensitivities and gut microbiome imbalances and use that data to create customized anti-inflammatory nutrition programs and gut restoration protocols.

By analyzing biomarkers, we design targeted interventions tailored to address specific requirements, encouraging optimal health and wellness. Adopting a diet packed with specific nutrients can enable your body to thrive.

Supplementation: Enhancing Nutrition

In today's world, nutritional deficiencies are quite common due to diet, lifestyle, and medication. Relying on diet alone is often insufficient to achieve optimal nutrient status, especially with the Standard American Diet (SAD), which is truly representative of its acronym. The overwhelming availability of processed foods sets the stage for a lifetime of nutrient deficiencies and their correlating symptoms and health conditions. Introducing evidence-based supplements into your wellness routine provides much-needed nutrients for vitality and resilience.

Keep in mind that supplements should be used to complement a healthy lifestyle and diet by addressing nutrient requirements and supporting bodily functions that may be compromised. Carefully chosen supplements can be very beneficial for your overall health and can be tailored to your specific health condition. Examples of such supplements include Vitamin D, methylated Vitamin B12 and Folate, omega-3 fatty acids, probiotics, and antioxidants. As mentioned earlier with micronutrient testing, genetic tendencies, methylation pathways, enzyme activity, and metabolic inefficiencies are learned through proper lab work, which determines supplementation regimens to treat, delay onset, or even prevent disease.

Various scientific investigations highlight the benefits of tailored supplementation in improving health outcomes and reducing the risk of diseases. For example, a recent comprehensive analysis of three large-scale studies showcases the effects of omega-3 fatty acid supplementation on health, such as significantly lowering cardiovascular disease risks and incidents (Kris-Etherton et al., 2019). Utilizing appropriate supplements enhances the body's ability to prevent disease, heal, and revitalize.

Moreover, supplementation serves as an approach to combat the impacts of environmental pollutants, oxidative stress, and lifestyle factors that accelerate aging and chronic illnesses. By strengthening your body's antioxidant defenses and aiding in detoxification, you can increase your resistance to life stressors, preserving your health and well-being for years to come. In recent years, supplement manufacturing technology has advanced significantly, and the science behind the specific nutrients and extracts used in supplements has improved as well. Today, there are supplements available with proven clinical benefits to aid in almost every stage of life, disease, and prevention to help extend your health span, not just your lifespan.

Keeping active; Embracing the Richness of Motion

Engaging in physical activity is essential for a healthy life. It can revitalize your mind and body. Choose exercises that match your interests and objectives. For example, take brisk walks in nature, lift weights at the gym, or practice yoga at home. Maintaining a routine and finding joy in moving your body is most important, developing a connection with your body's natural abilities. Consistent exercise has the greatest benefits. Even if you are short on time and/or low in energy, find a way to move your body. Start with just a few minutes and go from there.

Numerous scientific studies emphasize the benefits of physical activity in enhancing overall health and well-being. A comprehensive analysis published in The Lancet underscores that decreased mortality rates are linked to higher levels of physical activity (Ekelund et al., 2016). By embracing an active lifestyle, you nurture resilience, energy, and longevity while unlocking your body's rich potential.

Functional movement assessments can help identify imbalances, postural issues, or movement inefficiencies that may increase your risk of injury or negatively affect your performance. By addressing these root causes through exercises and physical therapy, you can improve your balance, enhance your functional capabilities, and reduce the likelihood of musculoskeletal problems. Injuries often occur when people lack coordination and confidence. Therefore, it is recommended to perform slow, deliberate, and precise movements with proper form, which can provide early benefits and help you safely progress in your exercise routine.

Beyond these benefits, staying active can also enhance mental clarity and emotional stability. Movement is an element of biology crucial for sustaining optimal function and energy levels throughout one's life. Regular exercise triggers the release of endorphins, chemicals that boost feelings of happiness and wellness. Embracing movement helps you feel more connected to yourself and the world around you, promoting a sense of richness, filled with vitality and contentment.

Meditation: Cultivating Inner Richness

Meditation serves as a sanctuary from the chaos of life, allowing you to nurture inner peace and spiritual harmony. By incorporating meditation into your daily routine, you can build resilience, find peace, and achieve an emotional balance that enhances every aspect of life, cultivating a sense of inner abundance and spiritual satisfaction. Dedicate moments each day to quieting your thoughts, practicing mindfulness, and connecting with yourself. If you're new to meditation and wondering where to start, explore techniques, such as breathing exercises or guided visualization to find what resonates best.

There is a significant amount of evidence supporting the positive impact of meditation on emotional and mental health. A study published in JAMA Internal Medicine revealed that mindfulness meditation can greatly reduce anxiety, depression, and pain (Goyal et al., 2014). Another study more recently published in the American Journal of Hypertension investigated the effects of Transcendental Meditation (TM) on blood pressure, psychological distress, and coping in young adults. Results showed significant improvements in blood pressure, anxiety, depression, anger/hostility, and coping (Nidich Sl, et al., 2009). These studies add to the growing body of evidence supporting the effectiveness of meditation as a tool for enhancing mental health and physical well-being.

Here's a simple breathing exercise to try on your own. The 4-7-8 breathing technique, developed by Dr. Andrew Weil, is an easy and effective method for meditative breathwork.

- Begin by exhaling completely through your mouth.
- Now, inhale quietly through your nose for a count of four: 1...2...3...4
- Hold your breath for a count of seven: 1...2...3...4...5...6...7
- Then exhale audibly through your mouth for a count of eight: 1...2...3...4...5...6...7...8

Repeat this cycle for four breaths, gradually extending the duration as you become more comfortable with the practice. It's ok if you struggle with the timing. Just try to keep the rhythm to realize the benefits. Work your way up to 8 breathing cycles if using it to help you fall asleep. The physiologic benefits of this practice begin to occur just after the first breathing cycle, which is only nineteen seconds. This rhythmic breathing pattern has been shown to regulate heart rate variability and blood pressure, which induces relaxation, calms the nervous system, and promotes mental clarity and emotional equilibrium. Although very relaxing, this type of practice can be used any time of day when you have a few minutes to focus.

I have even done this while out walking the dog and used my steps as the counting method. Give it a try for a few days; it can be surprisingly therapeutic.

Hormone Optimization: Balancing the Richness of Healthy Aging

As we age, optimizing our hormones becomes crucial to maintaining our health and vitality. Comprehensive hormone tests assessing sex hormones, adrenal hormones, thyroid hormones, and metabolic markers offer insights into endocrine health. They can reveal any imbalances or irregularities that negatively impact your health and vitality. By identifying the root causes, tailored interventions such as bioidentical hormone replacement therapy (BHRT), lifestyle adjustments, and dietary changes can be implemented to restore hormonal balance and enhance your vitality, energy levels, body composition, motivation, sexual function, and libido as you grow older. This approach helps to address any unique variances and ensures hormonal balance, allowing us to experience life to its fullest.

Research highlights the role of hormone optimization in supporting health and vitality throughout life. For instance, studies published in The Journal of Clinical Endocrinology & Metabolism illustrate how optimized testosterone levels lead to improvements in body composition, metabolic functions, and quality of life for men (Snyder et al., 1999 & 2016). Another recent study published in the Journal of Prescribing Practice investigated menopausal symptoms and overall health in women who received individualized BHRT. Results demonstrated 52% increase in quality of life and significant reductions in 21 menopause associated symptoms. (Martins et al., 2020). Optimizing your hormones can help you regain energy, resilience, and enthusiasm for life while embracing every moment with renewed zest.

In Closing; A Path to Health & Riches

I've learned that life's richness isn't a destination. It's a continual journey of self-discovery and personal growth, a journey through which we uncover the depths within ourselves. I encourage you to approach the journey with an open mind and a sense of wonder, understanding that true wealth comes from within, regardless of circumstances or recognition. Be thankful for the abundance surrounding you, and ground yourself in the moment, cherishing each breath, heartbeat, and precious instance of life.

For anyone struggling to navigate the maze of misinformation regarding longevity, it is advisable to seek the guidance of an experienced healthcare professional to determine what best suits your individual biochemistry. Functional health is the thread that infuses richness into every aspect of our existence, allowing us to fully experience life without physical, mental, or emotional restrictions. By caring for our bodies through diet, exercise, supplements, meditation, and hormones, we unleash our potential for vitality and well-being. Embrace this path with respect and purpose, as good health holds the key to unlocking life's richness in all its beauty.

***

In health and vitality,

Ryan Lombardo, DAOM, ABAAHP, BCIM

To contact Tyan:

t: 847.905.0440

e: connect@thelongevityexchange.com

w: TheLongevityExchange.com

References:

- Ekelund, U., et al. (2016). Does Physical Activity attenuate, or even eliminate, the detrimental association of sitting time with mortality? A harmonized meta-analysis of data from more than 1 million men and women. *The Lancet*, 388(10051), 1302–1310.

- Estruch, R., et al. (2018). Primary Prevention of Cardiovascular Disease with a Mediterranean Diet Supplemented with Extra-Virgin Olive Oil or Nuts. *The American Journal of Clinical Nutrition*, 108(3), 523–533.

- Goyal, M., et al. (2014). Meditation Programs for Psychological Stress and Well-being: A Systematic Review and Meta-analysis. *JAMA Internal Medicine*, 174(3), 357–368.

- Martins V. et al. (2020). Compounded Bioidentical HRT Improves Quality of Life and Reduces Menopausal Symptoms. *Journal of Prescribing Practice* 2020 2:7, 384-390.

- Kris-Etherton PM, et al. (2019). Recent Clinical Trials Shed New Light on the Cardiovascular Benefits of Omega-3 Fatty Acids. Methodist Debakey Cardiovasc J. 2019 Jul-Sep;15(3):171-178.

- Nidich Sl, et al. (2009). A randomized controlled trial on effects of the Transcendental Meditation program on blood pressure, psychological distress, and coping in young adults. *Am J Hypertens*. 2009 Dec;22(12): 1326-31.

- Snyder, P. J., et al. (2016). Effects of Testosterone Treatment in Older Men. *Journal Clin Endocrinol & Metab*, 101(1), 354–363.

- Snyder, P.J., et al. (1999). Effect of Testosterone Treatment on Body Composition and Muscle Strength in Men Over 65 Years of Age. *Journal Clin Endocrinol & Metab*. 1999;84: 2647-53.

Princess Merrilee of Solana Ph.D
Ambassador of Love

Author | Mentor | Advocate

Merrilee's journey to love began in 2009 with a commitment to love as a characteristic of Being to experience the life God promised to deliver.

Award-Winning, International Best-Selling Author, Mentor, and Advocate for Love, Merrilee demonstrates how to implement the *Power of Love* to solve any problem, dilemma, or concern.

Board Advisor: Dream Changers Publishing. Star Force Commander Princess Merrilee in comic books, event centers, radio, and movies.

Podcast Host: The Merrilee Show, HIGH in the CANOPY with Dr. John LaCasse, and The Rich Code Club. Co-author: Cracking the Rich Code, volumes one, four, nine, and thirteen. I Am Still Here and The Change 16.

Awards & Recognition: Marquis Who's Who, The Wall Street Journal, and Millennium Magazine, Queen Crown: Princess Merrilee of Solana, Guardian of Divinity, annex the Marsich Crown Kingdom. International Impact Award. Nobel Peace Prize nominee (2024) THE GAME, Winning by Virtue One Move at a Time.

Books featuring Merrilee:

Deals Danger Destiny and Floppy Feathers by Dr. John LaCasse. Knowing Merrilee, My Life with a Princess, by Craig Lipscomb.

Merrilee attributes all of her success to the Glory of God.

Website: merrileeofsolana.com

Learn THE GAME | Join the Castle Community | Schedule Private Lessons.   LoveMastery.me

To Love and Be Loved in Return
By Princess Merrilee of Solana

When talking about business, the topic of love is rarely included. Love is typically reserved for private affairs, having no place in the boardroom. After all, how does love increase our bottom line?

Most business professionals agree that if there is to be a trajectory of expansion and growth, business must involve planning, procedures, goals, filing, reporting, acquiring, contracts, applications, pitches, marketing, research, accounting, and a close attention to the numbers. I didn't like the sound of that. Even when earning my business degree, it was all so burdensome.

My decision to go back to school was an act of *self-love;* an investment in me. That's all. I had no plan of how I would use my degree. It wasn't the course of study that would dictate my future, it was *the people.* My classmates proved to be my greatest assets. They saw me and *loved me*. Their words of encouragement, support, friendship, and respect, as well as their naming me "The Show" taught me about me.

After graduation, I continued to invest in myself, becoming an avid reader and advocate for saying yes to opportunity and suggestion from people I met along the way who had my best interest at heart. Like a child, I was open to receiving the gift without reservation. I was thankful for everyone who would invest in me, add progress to my path, and show me how to become a better version of myself.

Becoming a better version of myself meant to me that I could be committed to love no matter the circumstance. I would love my way through it.

To love became my profession. I surrendered the common perception of chasing a dollar, to allow my novel profession the opportunity to create success with each test presented. Each test gave me an opportunity to overcome my challenges without causing pain to another.

My behavior communicated like an antenna. I sent love into the universe, and the universe sent love in return with gifts I never see coming. Over the years, the one gift that has remained consistent is the coincidental timing of a penny. Every time I pass a test, or when I'm feeling especially grateful for my life, or when there's a specific message for me, a penny will appear out of nowhere. I truly believe that my focused attention on the Spirit of love has created a way for the other side to speak directly to me. Whatever it is, be it angels, guides, ascended masters, co-creators, aliens, the Galactic Federation or the Holy Spirit, something is definitely watching over me and communicating a direction for my success.

I trust our communication and allow it to direct my every move, completely enamored by our exchange. I'm experiencing a world where this unseen charitable language of love proves itself, even when the *real world* vies for control of my attention.

Controlling my attention would appear easy when the responsibility of home, family, and career demanded most of my time. In reality, I had a lot of opportunities to practice self-discipline. Through self-discipline, I learned how to love myself first and that, it turns out, is for the benefit of others. Loving my brother is literally as easy loving myself with honorable behavior. I mind my words carefully and the universe responds by showing me what is true, and people show me what isn't true. Although it hurts, I've learned to let it go and find ways to love harder.

Finding ways to love harder became a game. On the offense, I would proactively create situations that would extend my love to others, and on the defense, I would be careful to watch my words to avoid being the cause of my brother's pain. This ebb and flow observation of playing with the field of possibility kept me focused in "prayer" all day and all night. Moment to moment I had to make sure I was prioritizing people before process like work, dishes, phones, and my to do list. My first priority was to create value in myself to recognize value in others.

Creating value in myself stretched beyond education, reading, courses, and collecting evidence of my accomplishments. The value I sought was love. I had to become worthy of it. So, I focused on creating memories for others where I was the common denominator. This kind of commitment reaches further than being nice, kind, or considerate. Although these are appreciated, they are weak compared to the power of the imagination that lies within me. I had to love harder. Loving harder requires me to be present, recognize opportunity, lose my fear, and act in a virtuous way where my discipline is recognized by others.

My daughter Emma and I were in the Marshall's parking lot when a tall, young, tired-looking man selling candy bars asked if we would like to make a purchase.

"How much are they?" I asked.

"Three dollars," he said.

So, I rummaged through my bag to find three dollars. Just enough for one bar. I handed him the money, and he gave me one candy bar. We then walked to the car, continuing our conversation about our purchase from Marshalls.

"Emma?" I asked, interrupting my own thoughts.

"Hm?" She asked curiously, knowing I was up to something but not sure what.

"I found more money! Look!" I exclaimed as I reached into the center console of the car for my secret stash of just-in-case-I-can-make-a-universe-deposit money.

"Mom?" Emma asked quizzically, knowing something was up but not sure exactly what.

With that, I drove us back in search of the candy man, who was still standing on his perch, peddling his wares with the lackluster effort of someone standing in the sun two hours longer than they wanted to. Rolling the window down, I leaned out of the window and said with more excitement than before.

"Look! We found more money!" Before he could finish processing what I'd said, I handed him the money to purchase three more chocolate bars.

The drive home was short, full of laughter and our regular mother-daughter exchanges about the day, about life, and anything that fancied our interest. But I wasn't finished with the candy man yet. Searching for my other purse, which I found in short order. I decided to see if Emma was up for an adventure.

"Let's go back!" I said to her with a knowing smile, and as usual, Emma knew she was in for an adventure, something we both loved to experience together. So off we went with a plan to make his day.

We found him in the same spot, looking like it was his worst day ever.

"Look!" I said, giving him only a moment to recognize us, "We found more money!"

By now, he was looking at both of us like we were crazy.

"How many bars do you have?" I asked cheerfully as he opened his box of candy and started counting. He finally stopped at twenty-five bars and gave me the total. For added suspense, I made a show of counting my money in front of him, and then, upon finding the amount needed, I said, "I have it, we'll take them all!" with sheer delight.

Emma laughed, already knowing what we were up to, but seeing his reaction… made it all the more worthwhile. I don't think he had ever experienced such excitement over a box of candy bars, and it's unlikely he thought his day would end before lunch. When we got home, the boys and their friends were wondering why we had so many chocolate bars displayed proudly on the shelf for no special occasion or season.

"They are all for you!" I said, answering the unasked question and bringing smiles to all their faces.

During the holiday season, my best friend, her boyfriend, another friend, and I were ice skating at the Mission Inn in Riverside. It was late and freezing by the time we were leaving. As we were walking to the car, trying to keep warm, we noticed a homeless man sleeping on the steps of a church. I turned to our group and suggested we take a trip to Target to get him a few things. In the car, thanks to GPS, we discovered that Target was a good twenty-minute drive out of our way. No matter, I was on a mission.

Brent decided to join me at Target while the other two stayed warm in the car. He pushed the shopping cart, while I led the way through the aisles, tossing in what I felt were essentials. I quickly made a short list of items as we passed them: a pillow, a down blanket, a toothbrush, Oh and definitely toothpaste, a hairbrush, and a water bottle…

"Merrilee! Where is he going to put all this stuff?" Brent asked, interrupting my thoughts.

"That's a good question…" I offered and continued up the aisle. "I don't know," and I continued placing things in the basket: snacks, a Starbucks card, water, socks…

Brent kept trying to talk some sense into me, concerned for my nonsensical charity, but he was missing that the homeless man had gone to sleep without anything but what we saw him with, which wasn't much. A few people may have passed him that day and given him a dollar or the leftovers from their lunch…. But by the time he woke up, those gifts would be forgotten, and he'd be cold, hungry, and wanting again. We were creating something for him that would last longer and leave him better than we found him. And because I was directing the whole mission, it would also be humorous.

By the time we reached the checkout, his eyes nearly bulged out of his head. He couldn't believe the total I was about pay for this stranger's items. When we got to the car, he told the others in disbelief what he'd just witnessed. Thirty minutes later, we were silently placing the pillow, blanket and other purchases carefully on and around the man like a fairy godmother in the night. Finally, we concluded filling the Starbucks bag with the gift card, nuts, water bottle, and a little cash too. We stood in silence briefly to see if the man would wake up so we could greet him with his surprise. Apparently, the man had been too tired to wake up, so we hugged each other and smiled at our good job, then left as he lay there sleeping.

Although this man was the beneficiary of our generosity, the gift was for us. We made a beautiful memory we can all share.

Now don't get me wrong, love is not that easy. Love is serious when others push the boundary and attempt to cause pain. I am extra careful about how I proceed with those who demonstrate unloving behavior. I slow down, being careful to maintain my honor when assumptions cause others to draw conclusions without first asking questions.

Years of moment-to-moment practice taught me how to love no matter what the dilemma or circumstance. And when there wasn't a dilemma or challenging situation, I focused on what made me happy; birds singing, music, grounding, sun-gazing, and walking amongst the trees. I found nature was the easiest way to increase my temperance and my patience.

It was more than ten years of a conscious effort not causing pain to my brother by holding my boundary and standard of behavior, when I finally met John LaCasse. I had no idea the gift this man would turn out to be. A true gift. One that I could never buy or reciprocate what he was about to do for me. A gift like John could only be explained as love returned as promised.

The first time I heard his voice on social audio, his tone was humble, very humble compared to the depth and breadth of his education and experience. Getting to know each other brought many discoveries that would later serve a bigger story.

Unbeknownst to me, he was connecting all of his years of study with what he saw in me. For me, I was enjoying our friendship until later it became undeniably clear just how accomplished he was. This unassuming man of many years with the harmonic voice, was known as the "king of counter trade" a mega yacht broker, a university professor, deep sea diver, motorcycle enthusiast, and hunter who slept inside the carcass of an elk And that's just the beginning. Captain John LaCasse Ph.D., MBA walked away from a multi-million-dollar lifestyle to go back to school at fifty-nine. His circle of comrades included mobsters, Italian banking families, and handshakes with figure heads from China. John LaCasse wore long black cars and jet planes like Adidas. Fast cars in the driveway, massive houses with helipads, and big money deals without caution. He was the badass of Seattle whose reputation had him holding millions of dollars in a Burluti French leather briefcase. Celebrities like Jaques Cousteau, Stephen Hawking, and Valerie Taylor, along with presidents, diplomats, university Chancellors, and students who knew that he was the wild card; unpredictable, yet totally capable of getting the job done.

His association with Harvard, The University of Maryland, The George Washington University, The Society of Navel Architects &

Marine Engineers, The Cambridge University Press International Baccalaureate, Marquis Who's Who, The Golden Key International Honour Society, Kappa Delta Pi International Honor Society in Education, and the American Association of University Professors still don't speak to his pedigree vernacular of science, religion, astrology, social science, aviation, and mythology. Oh, and did I mention that he studied in Paris with Aquinas at Shakespeare And Company? My new friend was accomplished beyond measure.

> *No eye has seen*
>
> *No ear has heard*
>
> *No mind has conceived*
>
> *What God has prepared for those who love him.*
>
> *1 Corinthians 2:9*

I had no idea what God had prepared as the legendary John LaCasse, would later be divinely commissioned as witness and scribe to convey my story.

John's story begins with Deals Danger Destiny. A memoir that later morphs into my story in Floppy Feathers. Together, they rewrite history and events, inspiring hope and direction for future generations. The gift delivered, as promised.

On the heels of John's book, I learned that "Knowing Merrilee, My Life with a Princess, by Craig Lipscomb had been funded against all odds and was set to publish. The timing was perfect without intention. John writes my story and Craig follows up as witness. Never in a million years could I have imagined, planned, or predicted how enormously magical my life would be when I committed to love.

Making a lot of money either by corporate or entrepreneur is not exactly extraordinary, because money will never be more valuable than the delivery of a promise. I want the gift.

The gift is knowing my future is promised.

Looking back, I don't want to see the heartache, regrets, and apologies that were never said. I want to see the hugs, kisses, and words of appreciation I left along the way. My days will be spent wisely with family and friends who appreciate my existence. I want all the gifts I can experience because I choose to love first.

I will not cause pain to my brother. I'm a team player.

The absence of pain is responsible for my success. My ability to navigate through adversity, challenge, and dilemma without hurting anyone has blessed me with a gift that inspires others to love in return.

Craig also made a commitment not to cause pain. He joined me, observed my every move, watched me navigate through people and circumstances and declared, "I want to learn *this game!*" For the next seven years he focused on the same conviction to not cause pain. It wasn't easy.

He's been tested with people and dangerous circumstances that called for every virtue to be played. He held on, refusing to crack under pressure. With promise and perseverance, he learned how to let go and let the power of love solve his dilemmas. Now, he's not only witness to who I am, but he is also the example of the one who gains favor by following the instruction.

The moral of the story; anyone can experience an extraordinary life filled with favor that leads to success. For us, it was love that gave us our greatest gifts. I never imagined that I would write an award-winning book that could potentially unify humanity with a clear instruction on how to love. John had no idea that he would meet a woman who would be the living example of his years of knowledge and experience and would later inspire him to write an epic story to bridge the gap between the heavens and earth. And Craig, he was just trying to get by and get along when everything changed the moment, he committed to love himself first. The man he used to be is no longer recognizable.

I must stress that I had no plan for where I am today. I only followed the instruction to love.

All Glory be to God.

Princess Merrilee of Solana

***

To contact Merrilee:

MerrileeofSolana.com

LoveMastery.me

The Game, Winning by Virtue One Move at a Time by Princess Merrilee of Solana (2023)

DEALS DANGER DESTINY and Floppy Feathers by John LaCasse (2023-2024)

Knowing Merrilee, My Life with a Princess by Craig Lipscomb (2024)

Deena Giordano Ullom

Deena blends empathy, compassion, and intuition into a powerful force for organizational and personal growth. With a keen eye for potential, Deena excels in nurturing leadership qualities and fostering environments where clients can embrace and realize their full capabilities.

Her mission extends beyond traditional legal counsel; she is dedicated to guiding leaders in creating enduring legacies, fostering cultures of excellence, and aligning their operations with a purpose that transcends profit. This holistic approach is delivered through a suite of services that include legal advice, leadership coaching, consulting, appreciative inquiry facilitation, organizational development, and strategic planning.

Deena's academic and professional journey is marked by distinction. She earned her bachelor's degree magna cum laude and as Valedictorian from Kent State University, followed by a juris doctorate from Case Western Reserve University. Her commitment to excellence is further evidenced by certifications in coaching, mediation, conflict resolution, and executive leadership. A member of the Ohio Bar, she is also a Board-Certified Leadership & Executive Coach.

Outside the professional sphere, Deena is deeply invested in personal growth and wellness. She holds both 200-hour and 300-hour certifications in Yoga and Yoga Psychology. An avid yoga practitioner, nature enthusiast, reader, and lifelong learner, she finds joy in the simple pleasures of life.

Above all, Deena treasures time with her family, drawing strength and inspiration from her role as the proud mother of an 11-year-old son.

Awakening the Giant: A Journey Beyond Limiting Beliefs

By Deena Giordano Ullom

I was lying in my bed in my small bungalow in Garfield Heights, Ohio, on a beautiful summer evening. I was fourteen years old and was taking a mental inventory of my life. I was deeply in awe of how wonderful it was. I had a close-knit group of friends; my parents were getting back together after being divorced for much of my childhood, and I was a good athlete- captain of the cheerleading squad and played volleyball, softball, and basketball. I was in the student council and an "A" student at a school I loved. I was truly feeling happy and grateful. And just like that, my throat descended into my stomach, and I had a horrible sinking feeling that something awful was going to happen. This is not my life- it's too good. Something bad is lurking.

I did not immediately remember those thoughts the next morning, but that evening, my mom wanted to talk to me. And there it was- my mom's cancer had returned. She was diagnosed with breast cancer when I was ten and was in remission for four years. Not only was the cancer back, but it was back with a vengeance. She deteriorated over the next few months and died in February of my first year of high school.

I forgot about that night in my bedroom for many years, but the message was deeply ingrained: dreams were something I fantasized about or dreamt about, but not something that came true. It was like I allowed myself a threshold of happiness but did not dare to go too far- I couldn't handle another tragedy. Only what I didn't realize until much wasted time had passed was the tragedy of an unlived, unfulfilled life.

But why did I feel unworthy of a great life in the first place?

I distinctly remember being six years old and having a eureka moment. I didn't have words for it, just a "knowing." It took several decades to realize that's how my intuition works- I don't have visions or voices; I just "know." Anyway, I was in my room again (my room was my safe place, so I spent a lot of time there as a child) and realized I had outgrown my mom. My mom struggled with mental illness and was quite childlike. There was something about me that irked her. My guess is she thought having a child was going to be like having a doll- they're cute and low maintenance, and you can make them do whatever you want. However, that's not quite how I was. I was outspoken, smart, confident, and extremely independent. That didn't work for her, so she criticized me incessantly to keep me beneath her. From the time I woke up in the morning to the time I went to bed, there was a problem with just about everything I did. That day, when I was six, I "knew" what was happening and "knew" that being compliant would help quell the criticism. I stayed in my room or out of the house as much as possible.

When I wasn't alone, I spent a lot of my childhood trying to get my dad's attention (mostly unsuccessfully). My dad isn't a bad guy; kids just really weren't his thing. Unfortunately, getting attention from my dad didn't work that well. We all adopt coping mechanisms to deal with the hard things in life. My coping mechanism was achieving. Every time I received an "A" on a test or received an "at-a-girl" from my coaches or was praised for stepping up and leading, I felt ok- I felt worthy of taking up air in this world.

We also operate under a set of beliefs formed early in life. The set of beliefs I formed from these early experiences were:

> 1. Don't be too happy, or something horrible will happen.
>
> 2. Stay small, so you don't threaten people with insecurities.
>
> 3. You are worthy as long as you achieve.

And this is how I survived for decades of my life. I set my life up so that I could only experience a certain amount of happiness, where I shrunk in the face of anyone that might be threatened by any part of me, and I worked myself to exhaustion trying to achieve so that I had worth.

When I was fourteen years old, I decided I wanted to be an attorney. I deeply wanted to be of service—to uphold truth and seek fairness. I graduated from elementary school and high school with honors and from college at the top of my class. I achieved the heck out of school while remaining mostly under the radar and turning down many great dream-come-true opportunities, including an internship on Capitol Hill and studying in Guadalajara.

As I entered law school, I had many serious health issues. I later realized the health issues were all manifestations of my painful and lonely childhood that were pent up and never expressed. Regardless, I graduated from law school, and soon after, I was hired for my dream job- as a county prosecutor. I was over the moon. The only thing I had to do was pass the three-day grueling bar exam. After eleven years, I was inches from achieving my "dream" of being a lawyer. Oh, but remember, dreams are not meant to come true for me. For the first time in my entire life, I failed. I did not pass the bar exam test. All my friends did. I was horribly ashamed and devastated. The day I found out was the second worst day of my life besides my mom dying. I lost my dream job as a prosecutor, and I spent the next few months without a job and studying again for that grueling test. Looking back, I'm pretty sure I sabotaged myself from passing the exam. Six months later, I passed the test and finally became an attorney- although not as a prosecutor. I gained a lot of skills as a defense attorney, but I wanted to pursue my original dream. I was hired at a prosecutor's office and was so excited and proud. In this county, prosecutors had to do rotations through the different divisions until they reached the criminal division. I breezed through the first two divisions with flying colors. I was weeks away from moving to the criminal division, but I did it again, I sabotaged it. I was again experiencing some health issues, and I asked my supervisor to hold me back until I resolved them. A few weeks later, out of nowhere and even as a surprise to me, I accepted a job in a city two-and-a-half hours from my home in an area I knew absolutely nothing about. I became a General Counsel for a charter school even though I did not even know what a charter school was. I worked hard, figured it out, had much success in this role, and became the Director of Human Resources, which was another area I knew nothing about. What I did realize is that the better people were treated and the clearer the expectations and communications were, the less legal work I had to do!

Although I loved my job, I left it to move to Chicago to be with my soon-to-be-husband. Although I was excited to start a new life with my fiancée and his kids, I left behind a job and home that I loved, as well as all my friends. I was happy in my new relationship but sad to leave everything else behind. It was as if I believed I couldn't have it all.

In the meantime, I had started a yoga practice- not willingly, because all that woo-woo stuff wasn't for me- I was too logical and was not very in touch with my feminine energy. I remember in one of my first classes, the beautiful yoga teacher told us to fold over and drop our thoughts. I remember saying to myself, "drop my thoughts??? Where in the f*@k am I supposed to put them??!!" I didn't even know not thinking was an option! However, I kept showing up on my mat, and each time, it cracked me open a bit more. I went from a closed-off analytical person who was much more in touch with my masculine energy, to a loving, empathic, and intuitive person who was claiming her divine feminine energy. Only after I was in touch with this gentler, softer version of myself (plus a lot of therapy) did I receive my greatest gift- my son. The moment I gave birth and held my son in my arms, my entire world turned upside down. My son looked at me with such pure love in his eyes- for no reason at all that I had no choice but to finally begin to release my long-held belief that I had to "achieve" to have worth. He was my little miracle. I wasn't cured, but I was making progress.

Despite this, I still had other limiting beliefs I had to tackle. I remember attending networking events with such accomplished people, and I always felt so envious and inferior. I beat myself up incessantly about not being an "expert" as I had become somewhat of a generalist. Part of the reason for not reaching any real success in the profession I worked so hard to become part of is that my "me-ness" always offended someone- usually my superiors. I would initiate and execute transformational endeavors for my employers, and although, at first, I would be met with praise, I would soon start to be criticized and nit-picked for just about everything I did. In response, I would work hard and feverishly to get back in their good graces. And I would try not to shine so as not to upset them. It was like an amalgamation of my mother's criticism and my father's lack of attention all in one- over and over again.

With each position, I learned to recognize quicker what was happening when I went from the "Golden Child" to "Black Sheep." Reflecting on my relentless pursuit of my dad's attention, I realized a pivotal truth: seeking validation from others was a mirror reflecting my own insecurities. This epiphany wasn't immediate but emerged through introspection and therapy. It marked a turning point, teaching me the power of self-validation and the importance of looking inward for approval. I attached less to how they treated me and reacted less to the criticisms, but I would stay in these positions out of a desire for security- that is until I had my last straw.

I took a position as General Counsel even though my gut was warning me against it- I justified it due to the security it could bring our family. However, my boss in this position was without question the worst boss I have ever encountered. The turnover rate in her department was 247% if that tells you anything. Anyway, I quickly went from rockstar to has-been. One Friday afternoon, she sent me a scathing email about my lack of leadership for not agreeing with her about her choice to terminate a good employee on my team. My old response would be to crumble and apologize- not on this day. On this day, I smiled. Finally, I was pushed too far. Without a Plan B, I resigned. I no longer was going to stand for poor treatment- either of myself or anyone else in an organization. I wasn't put on this earth to shrink; I need to shine and illuminate the path for others.

In accepting the General Counsel position against my intuition's warning, I confronted a universal struggle: the tension between security and authenticity. This decision became a powerful lesson in trusting my inner voice—a lesson that resonates far beyond career choices. It prompted me to ask, "Where else in my life am I ignoring my intuition for the illusion of security?" This question invites us all to consider the areas in our lives where we might be compromising our true selves for comfort.

Throughout my corporate legal career, I also led the HR/People departments. Through my voracious curiosity and love of learning, I consumed books, certifications, and courses on strengths-based leadership, organizational development, and employee engagement. I realized how much I love being part of the transformation of a business into a better version of itself, but I was equally, if not more, infatuated with the massive transformation possible through strengths-based growth and development of leaders and employees. I eventually received my coaching certification through Case Western Reserve University and became a Board-Certified Leadership and Executive Coach. Weeks before I resigned from that last position, I read a book called "The Healing Organization" by Raj Sisodia. I became inspired to work with companies who feel a deep calling to discover their purpose beyond profit.

Even though I intellectually knew that tragedy doesn't strike when my life is going well, there was still the fourteen-year-old girl residing inside me who wasn't so sure- that night's message haunted her for years. This time, I chose to confront this belief head-on. Instead of succumbing to the familiar narrative of self-doubt, I actively visualized succeeding in this endeavor, transforming my fear into focused determination. This shift wasn't just about starting a business; it was a profound moment of overcoming the deep-seated belief that I didn't deserve my dreams.

I took a leap and began to step into my calling; my deepest professional desire- to help leaders and companies thrive. And just like that, the universe opened its doors. Serendipity arrived at every turn. I took another leap and attended a Mastermind with an incredible brain trust of amazing people, including the founder of the style of yoga I had been practicing for the past twenty years- Baron Baptiste. It was a transformational experience, and I left there with an abundance mindset- knowing there were more companies to serve than I had capacity, so I partnered with my brilliant law school friend and colleague and started ThrivePoint Strategic Services to help small businesses build strong foundations and find their purpose beyond profit through strategic legal, human resources, organizational development support and advising, and executive coaching. I no longer resent my generalist background; instead, I feel proud of the breadth of knowledge I've acquired and continue to hone my intuition so I can help leaders and businesses faster. Also, after years of a struggling marriage, my husband and I are working to build a stronger foundation. Finally, I have the great privilege and honor of watching my eleven-year-old son grow and thrive. Life is good and I deserve it.

Psychological research underscores how our early experiences shape our belief systems, acting as lenses through which we view the world. This understanding illuminated my own journey, helping me see that the beliefs I formed in childhood—about happiness, self-worth, and achievement—were not edicts but hypotheses to be tested and revised. Embracing this perspective was liberating, offering a path to reframe my narrative.

So, what is the moral of this story? There is a formula for changing limiting beliefs. Awareness is the first step. One surefire way to gain awareness of a limiting belief is when you notice yourself in the same situation multiple times. Another way is when you do not feel fulfilled- like something is missing. The second, and most critical step in quashing limiting beliefs is taking massive action. My counselor once called me out when she told me, "You can read all the books about ice skating you want, but unless you put the skates on and get out on the ice, you'll never learn to skate."

As I stand at this point in my journey, aware of the paths I've traversed and the ones yet to unfold, I realize that the greatest transformation has been within. Overcoming limiting beliefs was not about achieving external success; it was about reclaiming my worth, my potential, and my power to shape my destiny. This journey is ongoing, a continuous process of learning, unlearning, and relearning.

I invite you to embark on your own journey of transformation. Start by identifying one limiting belief that has held you back. Ask yourself: What courageous action can I take today to challenge this belief?

Together, let's step into a future where we are not defined by our past, but empowered by our capacity to grow, change, and thrive.

As we share this human experience, remember that transformation is not a destination but a journey—one that we navigate together, learning, growing, and evolving. Within this journey lies an often-overlooked arena for change: the world of business. Through the lens of transformational leadership, businesses have the unique capacity to become catalysts for personal and collective growth. Imagine a workplace where overcoming limiting beliefs is not just encouraged but embedded in its culture—where everyone is seen for their potential to develop, grow, and utilize their strengths. Here, transformation becomes more than personal; it becomes a collective movement that thrives on the contributions of each member, creating a ripple effect that reaches far beyond its walls. This environment not only fosters personal triumphs but also paves the way for a world where we uplift each other, challenging the status quo and rewriting the narrative of what is possible. Your story, with all its challenges and triumphs, is a testament to your resilience and a beacon for this new dawn. Let's move forward with the courage to challenge our limiting beliefs, to support one another in our personal and professional growth, and most importantly, to believe in the endless possibilities of our collective transformation. Your story is waiting to be rewritten, within the pages of this new chapter where business and leadership are the vessels of change. Are you ready to take the pen?

***

To contact Deena:

Deena@thrivepoint-strategic.com

216-469-5781

Carole Stizza

Carole Stizza is an Executive Leadership Coach who gets leaders to identify and achieve elevated success. She has created a Leadership Development program for organizations as a pipeline for developing leaders at every level and has coached and trained a range of executives in global companies including Software, Tech, Legal, Healthcare, and Government Services.

As a military spouse, she spent her career studying the differences between corporate and military leadership, identifying the leadership ripple affects that achieve extraordinary results. She holds a Master's in Industrial-Organizational Psychology, is an international speaker, and best-selling author. She holds credentials with the International Coaching Federation and the Society of Human Resource Management.

Carole has received awards that include Top 10 Executive Coaches to Watch in 2023 by US Insider, Top 20 Leadership Development Coach in 2023 by HRTech, Woman of the Year, Volunteer of the Year, and her favorite: coolest 'Ya-Ya' from her young grandkids.

Carole is a contributing author of ***Compassion @ Work*** (2017) and ***Coach Wisdom Vol 1*** (2019), and in 2021, she published her first book: ***The Ask Framework: Questions that Elevate Your Influence, Leadership, and Performance.***

From Adversity to Advantage: Redefining Your Leadership Story

By Carole Stizza

My family filled my grandfather's new blue Chrysler Sedan as we returned from a funeral. Upon turning left towards the driveway, we were T-boned by a young driver racing his buddy over the hills near our family farm, killing my mother, grandmother, and grandfather, while injuring other family members, including my brother and me.

I was 6. I still remember every detail.

I awoke with a broken arm that posed a challenge in rolling down the side window. When I finally did manage to open the window and crawl out through the smoke of the overturned car, I am forever grateful that the scene of bodies I looked back upon was not gruesome. In my young mind, they all looked like they were sleeping, and I was certain that they would wake up as help arrived.

It was a crystal-clear blue day, and the sun was hot. As I sat nearby, I remember listening to the paramedics accounting for people in the car. They never mentioned my 3-year-old brother. I spoke up and asked a person near me where my brother was. I was brushed off. I persisted.

When a nurse finally heard me, she sent out the call to look for one more person. The tow truck stopped its work, everyone gathered back at the vehicle, and my brother was found jammed underneath the backseat bench, an unconscious child among all the coils and stuffing. I cannot fathom the outcome had I not persisted that day.

That accident is something I had buried deep. In my mind, that accident = tremendous loss. I grew up identifying as motherless, feeling as if I had been cheated, and angrily holding onto that identity as a badge of endurance.

I never considered the lessons I learned that day or how they shaped my behaviors until years later. As I started my coaching practice, I found myself listening to a speaker at a local conference. After sharing his own story of overcoming a huge challenge and how he now looks at that event, he turned to the audience and asked,

"Who do you get to become today, in the best way, due to the negative things that have happened to you?"

I had not realized until that question, how much I had held onto a childhood identity that no longer fit, held onto a story heavy with details I was tired of telling, and felt the burden of anger that needed to be released. The brilliance of giving my experience a positive narrative for who I've become filled me with a new perspective. I went from a story of loss to a story with purpose in mere hours.

I am never surprised, yet always in awe when a client achieves the same. The ripple effect of a new perspective changes everything.

Mastering the positive side of my stories has been a meaningful and transformative journey. I've seen it happen repeatedly for others, too.

A story's impact on self-awareness, new perspectives, transformative thinking, and resilience remains a large influence on everyone's daily habits.

Have you ever stopped to think about how your habits started? What stories influence those habits today?

This book is filled with chapters to inspire your perceptions surrounding wealth. The aim is for you to be more self-aware, action-oriented, and healthier in your pursuit of the richness you want in your life. Often, this includes money. For many, money is a huge trigger, especially leaders. Deadlines, projects, employee salaries, and take-home pay are all affected by perspectives and stories.

I remember watching my father squander money on short-term indulgences: cigarettes, alcohol, or eating out with friends. Then, he would rant when we asked for money for school needs: lunch money, clothing, instruments, or sports gear. Instead of teaching us how to manage money, he instilled in us a scarcity mindset around money. That story was stuck in my head for years and bled over into my parenting and work attitudes.

A scarcity mindset around money may influence you to feel you need to work to gain overtime pay, go on every trip you are assigned without question, or take on other people's work to gain attention. I know I did. How you work may all stem from a story around money that isn't healthy or well-informed. When a leader showcases any of these same beliefs or attitudes, it can hurt their teams. Which stories are attached to how you think about money?

Now, when I sit down with leaders to elevate their impact, we often end up identifying the stories that built them up and honor their journey, as well as the stories that hold them back, including those around finances. We go back and reflect to move forward, and we look at the hidden stories holding them back, because the ignored, forgotten, or buried stories often hold the most impressive rewards. This is a major contribution to **self-awareness.**

Stories from our past are important. We all developed skills and behaviors that helped us cope as we grew up. These behaviors were developed when we reacted to other people making the big choices for us, and we craved control. The stories attached to our actions are important because these behaviors are measured in our leadership.

Bob Anderson, co-author of Scaling Leadership, studied over one million leaders and found that few are completely equipped to handle everything thrown at them. Anderson discovered 11 reactive characteristics that can hold leaders back from achieving the great results they seek and 18 creative characteristics that can launch a leader into getting extraordinary results. Leadership 360 assessments often explore characteristics that are highly present. Without fail, the reactive characteristics are often limited to short-term success and attached to thinking that worked brilliantly earlier in their career and yet fails in long-term challenges.

The saying, 'What got you here, won't get you there," is alive and well.

And what you believe becomes your reality. **New perspectives** matter.

Dealing with a difficult and grieving father, I always thought of myself as someone who could read other people well because I endured his mood swings. Luckily, I've learned I'm wired that way, regardless of my father's shortcomings. However, when you are raised to make others happy, you can become an enabler by default, which comes at the expense of understanding one's own needs and boundaries. I became acutely aware of the benefits of being quiet, well-mannered, adaptable, and compliant to appease my dad's moods. It turned out that while these same behaviors impressed adults wherever I went as a young adult, trying to appease everyone came at the cost of improving my critical thinking for college.

Thankfully, my talent for psychology led me to study the ties between transformative thinking and behaviors. This research was foundational in facilitating change quickly. When you recognize you need something new, yet hold onto the old, your brain can feel like it's short-circuiting, waiting for you to realize you are stuck. This is where **transformation comes into play**.

Letting go of old stories is hard and makes it harder for change to stick. While stories connect you to the behaviors and habits you carry with you, changing the way you tell your stories is imperative for change to hold. When you can adapt your stories with new perspectives, the behaviors, and habits also adapt.

Connecting my experience with the speaker's message, I recognized:

- When you review events, you get to **choose** how you tell the story.
- When you **give credit for who you've become**, you balance out the emotions connected with the event.
- Who you get to become is a **choice, not fate.**

When **new perspectives** emerge, you have a choice of how to think differently.

I remember the moment a small dismissive gesture from a stranger drew me back to a moment in time in my childhood. A moment when feeling invisible deeply compromised my faith in feeling valued and worthy of love. Shortly after, sitting in a quiet office, I turned and read a quote that stopped me in my tracks.

"We accept the love we think we deserve."

The words 'accept' and 'we think we deserve' stood out. The moment I read it, I felt the shift. Like a giant stone dropped into a quiet lake, the water ripples stretching to the edges; new thinking took hold.

My understanding of what kept me questioning, pushing, and testing others to constantly prove that I was worth love became connected to that old childhood feeling. That childhood feeling held me back from thinking I deserved love, so I didn't accept it either. One small memory rippling in the undercurrent of my subconscious was pushing me to test the limits of my dearest relationships.

That single moment transformed how I could accept love instead of testing it.

Moments that transform happen in those quiet moments between the chaos of feelings. And those quiet moments are vital. Transformation, at its heart, is when you experience a shift in your thinking, that changes your perspective, enough to change your behaviors and make those changes stick. Make time for the quiet in the chaos. The ripple effect is real.

When Sue was a young mother, she smoked. Her kids tried in vain to figure out ways to make her stop. They even stooped to putting firecracker poppers in her cigarettes to explode when she lit up. Soon after, she witnessed her mother, a fellow smoker, have a heart attack. During recovery, the doctor told her mother directly, "This will continue to happen if you continue to smoke." Sue stopped smoking immediately and never smoked again, while her mother continued to smoke (for the rest of her life) and experienced a total of 7 cardiac events.

Transformation can happen in a second, or it can happen in a string of moments. These moments often occur when one is in the thick of things in their life, and Bam! The idea that had been simmering suddenly makes sense; the piece of data suddenly fits, and one sees how making a change matters to the desired results.

Sue's transformative decision happened in a moment. Others struggle. The National Institute of Medicine recognizes 5 stages of change: pre-contemplation, contemplation, preparation, action, and maintenance. When there is a relapse, those who coach often refer to this as either a re-commitment or an opportunity for goal clarity. Identifying what is behind the change is often connected to a story.

Sue's mother wanted to smoke, even with heart attacks looming. It was a part of her story she liked. Sue stopped smoking because she wanted different outcomes. Sue wanted to create a different story than her mother.

What you want matters to getting great results.

After receiving his debrief of a 360 assessment, Mike was puzzled as to why his people didn't recognize how often he complimented or cheered them on. There had been a gap in his assessment results where he had reported a high level of support and those who took part in his 360 reported a different experience. I suggested he pay attention to how people praise others around him.

Later, while watching one of his kids' baseball games, he heard the coach give positive, detailed support to one of his players. Mike recognized that while he would tell his folks they were doing great work, he failed to give specific recognition of what his people did to achieve that great work. The next day, he started providing detailed feedback on how he saw each person contribute to the group's success.

When we met again, he shared that he experienced higher energy with his team when he noticed their specific work contributions. He now recognized how specific and positive feedback provided the support that many had craved. He also recognized that because he had never received such specific praise himself, he hadn't permitted himself to do the same for those he led. His story in his head included, "If he hadn't received it, they didn't need it either."

Stories connect how your past influences how you move into your future and are worth evaluating, unpacking, and embracing as a gateway to growth. No one is more surprised than the client when their actions today stem from past stories they've forgotten for years. While uncomfortable memories aren't invited, they still surface when we look to understand the whole YOU. It is a part of your experiences, and experiences create leaders.

Leaders who experience anything positive or negative build **resilience**, especially in handling the next negative. In a twist of fate, the accident when I was 6 wasn't the only car accident or trauma I would face. I've survived, in total, 3 car accidents - all while stopped and turning left. Add to that a surprise stage 3 cancer diagnosis before age 50, and **resilience** mattered.

Resilience is the ability to keep getting back up. It is key in leadership, and getting back up is also the best way of showing up for yourself. We often hear of someone needing time to heal, deal, or adapt to a negative or traumatic event. There is truth in this. What we forget, is that it takes time, and we all need the grace to do that.

Few people tell us that **we get to decide** how we cope. Deciding *how* to get back up is solely motivated by the intent *to* get back up. Why and how you get back up, or even if you get back up, becomes the addition of adding resilience to your story.

Witnessing my father's grief steal his ability to get back up and lead effectively, I recognized the need for resilience in leadership. I also recognized a ripple effect of cause and effect in leadership results. Early in my career, whenever I found myself working under a leader who faltered, couldn't recover from a loss, or let their ego get in the way of better judgment, I recognized a ripple effect of discontent on employees. In contrast, being employed by a great boss created a positive ripple effect as they led with consistency, caring, vision, and respect for great communication. Add my time as a military spouse and executive coach, and I've now witnessed different ripple effects in corporate, government, and military leaders.

Executives are often too close to the day-to-day operations to recognize the ripple effect they create. Helping executives forecast the ripple effects opens new ways to think, decide, and evaluate if current ways of thinking will succeed. If the buck stops at the top, the top needs to know the ripple effect they have on the outcomes of those they lead. Especially, when turning failure into success. Getting back up after failure with the goal of success can feel monumental, but it is done day in and day out by many of our country's leaders.

Being a military spouse of a leader defending our nation's safety via space, I received a unique education on how successful breakthroughs are built upon failures.

When I finally saw the debris from where a rocket had exploded upon ignition, the launchpad was unrecognizable. The blast could have taken my husband's life or any of his crew. Brilliant minds and talent were now picking up the pieces of a multimillion-dollar program. The disbelief and grief were palpable.

It took time to choose how to heal, cope, and adapt. The failure became the motivation for the next launch to be successful, and when that next rocket successfully launched, the celebration was off the charts. Failure was foundational in that success story for every launch team member.

Few seek out failure, yet it is a part of the success equation, or success would not be recognizable. Leaders who become comfortable with failure adapt and build benchmarks to reach new success and tell new stories. Yet leaders are individuals who are challenged just like those they lead.

I have found that leaders embrace deeper self-awareness, new perspectives, transformative thinking, and stronger resilience because they want to transform their success in 4 different ways:

- Saving time = becoming more effective, efficient, or in control of time management.
- Saving money = retaining talent or achieving better outcomes for clients.
- Making money = gaining a promotion, attracting client projects, or higher quality of life.
- Increasing Influence = elevating communication skills and building better relationships.

Whether a leader aims to transform how they handle time, money, or influence, unpacking their story is key to understanding the ripple effect of change, especially when change is needed for the long haul. Creating more positive stories with deeper self-awareness, new perspectives, transformative thinking, and stronger resilience is important. They are key to reshaping how the brain reflects on the past and turns around to craft a better future.

I will always credit that first car accident for why I chose to speak up for my brother and why I get so much joy from helping people get results today. The bonus in my story: my brother, that unconscious, sweet 3-year-old boy, grew up to serve in the Marines for 20 years, deploying multiple times, and gifting the world with two sons.

Most leaders want to make a positive difference, develop their people, and be someone worthy of bragging about when not in the room. Great leaders understand that they only win when their people win. It becomes their legacy and part of their story.

If a leader's influence is not delivering this type of experience, the stories they hold onto are holding them back. That is the ideal time to elevate their self-awareness, introduce new perspectives, look for where transformative thinking is required, and evaluate resilience to transform those stories.

When looking to increase your success, do not hesitate to transform your leadership story. When needing a partner to do this, a coach is your secret weapon.

Written by Carole Stizza, Executive Leadership Coach

***

To contact Carole:

C: 719-351-5364

E: carole@relevant-insight.com

W: https://www.relevant-insight.com/

LK: https://www.linkedin.com/in/carolestizza/

IG: https://www.instagram.com/relevantinsightcoaching/

Steve Walsh

With over 25 years of consulting experience, Steve's journey commenced as an application developer specializing in Great Plains ERP software. Within Microsoft, Steve excelled in Dynamics 365 Finance and Operations consulting, culminating in his role as Global Support Program Manager, where he collaborated with Independent Software Vendors (ISVs) to deliver exceptional support solutions. Transitioning to partner channels, he established Customer Care programs and assumed the position of Delivery Director, overseeing technical and functional consultants for over a decade.

Now, as an Executive Coach for IT Leaders, Steve channels his extensive industry knowledge and coaching certifications from Dream University and the Canfield Training organization to empower IT professionals. His mission is to elevate productivity and job satisfaction through honing effective communication and leadership skills. Steve's commitment to ongoing professional development is underscored by his academic achievements, including a bachelor's degree in Computer Information Systems and an MBA in Technology Management.

By combining his wealth of experience with his passion for coaching, Steve is dedicated to helping IT leaders navigate challenges, seize opportunities, and achieve their career aspirations. Through personalized coaching sessions, he guides individuals toward personal and professional growth, fostering a culture of excellence and innovation within their organizations.

Breaking into Management
By Steve Walsh

Have you ever been passed up for a promotion? I certainly have on multiple occasions. It seemed like there was a key to a lock that I was missing. When I was in college, I worked at a movie theater for a couple of years. Going into my final year at college, I applied for the assistant manager job. Even though I felt I was the better candidate, a good friend got that job. It kept happening in several jobs after college.

When I worked for a global industry leader in software, I remember working long hours, taking risks, and earning technical certifications. All with the ambition that one day, I would be rewarded and move into the team leader position. As the months passed, our team grew rapidly with new team members. I thought that with the rapid growth and my new skills, I would be in a great position to be promoted. I watched other team members who were on the team for less than six months quickly move into management positions. This was highly frustrating, and I was at a loss.

I felt I was missing something. What was it? When I started to dig into this question, I started to read books on success, management, and other self-development concepts. I learned and grew a lot from a personal development standpoint. To give you context, I was a shy introvert with an analytical and technical mind. I was a typical computer programmer. In this chapter, I want to highlight three areas that were the keys to breaking through the management barrier. I also found that once you break the barrier, you may have to reset and break through the next management level. The three key areas that helped me the most were modeling, effective communication, and believing in myself.

One of the biggest lessons I learned was that people like to work with friends, people they know and can relate to. I was deep into the latest computer technologies and only talked about improving code. Some would say I was a classic nerd. I didn't fit the common mold of what a manager was. I was an outsider to the club. This was the challenge. Others had a hard time seeing me as a manager. They only saw me as a good computer programmer.

I learned it wasn't about me being a nerd but the others' perception of me. Upper management could not see me performing at the management level because they also couldn't relate to me. They could not recognize under all the technical jargon that I could lead people. They basically couldn't see themself at some level in me. Subconsciously the other managers couldn't see me sitting at the table and performing like they do. When I started to understand modeling, I overcame this hidden challenge, which was an essential component of success.

Modeling is when a person observes and imitates someone else's behavior. This can be seen in how someone dresses, how they start their day, what they talk about, what hobbies they have, how they interact with others, and so much more. Attention to detail is critical. Modeling is not losing who you are but learning from those around you who are in a position you would like to be.

I started by identifying the management team I wanted to join and be promoted to. I then started to observe and take notes of all the differences and commonalities in each person. I was also analyzing what I was doing and wasn't doing. I was creating a recipe for success.

After observing and taking notes on some of the managers' behaviors, I started to take some simple action steps. One of the first steps was to dress like the management team. When a manager visited our team, I noticed that they wore a blazer jacket, button-down shirts, and dress slacks. The technical team would generally wear short-sleeved collared shirts and Docker-style slacks. I also observed how they carried themselves and how they communicated.

Communication is a cornerstone to success. I worked on improving my communication skills in many ways, from taking additional grammar courses to joining Toastmasters. In general, this is an area I think everyone can always continue to improve upon. I put in the work and started noticing a difference in how upper management treated me. I was on the right path.

Have you ever wondered why some communications seem more effective than others? In my journey to break into management, I observed an instance where a manager simply did not understand communication and what was needed for a specific situation. This was very apparent in one meeting when a manager was looking for feedback on an off-track project. He was telling a long-drawn-out story, and no one was listening. It was his internal monologue, and people lost interest. To communicate his message and receive constructive feedback, he needed to have a dialogue with the team instead of a one-sided conversation. He also needed to understand the audience and communicate in such a way the team would be more interested in hearing his message. The project team was made up of software engineers, and the manager was more of an HR manager. This manager didn't take the time to speak in a manner that an analytical-minded audience would be receptive to.

To illustrate this further, if I were to broadcast my message on a 90.1 FM radio station, then everyone listening to 90.1 FM would hear my message. However, if the targeted audience I want to listen to my message is on 102.5 FM, then they will not hear my message simply because I am broadcasting on a different station. I will need to switch to 102.5 FM to be effective.

I figured out that we can categorize people into four basic personality types. A DISC assessment can help with this categorization. The four basic types are driver, influencer, support, and clarity. Each of these personality types communicates differently from the other. Understanding each type and how they primarily communicate can help you change the way you communicate with the other person's personality communication style.

For instance, my primary type or style of communication is clarity. I can talk to other clarity-type people all day long and be effective. However, I would not communicate effectively if I communicated from my natural clarity type to a driver type. Now, if I were to switch and communicate with a driver utilizing the driver's communication style, I would be more effective in that communication. In essence, I am switching radio stations to be more effective. Let's explore the four personality types as they relate to communication.

A driver type will generally be loud and direct. This type is very focused on getting to the goal, and they are not concerned about how they get there and who they talk over to get there. To communicate more effectively with a driver, I would be direct and factual without softening or sugarcoating the message. Many salespeople and organizational leaders score high in the driver category.

An influencer will generally be someone who shares enthusiasm when communicating. They are energetic, warm, and outgoing. They are people who like to have fun when interacting with people. To communicate with an influencer, I would be more energetic, smile more, and look for something to celebrate.

Someone who communicates with a support style is generally a humble person. They are naturally caring and look for ways to assist others. To communicate with a support type, I would take a soft approach. I would look for ways to show how my message will help everyone. To communicate effectively with a support type, I would keep it simple and show how they can assist with the situation.

Clarity types are analytical people. They need methods, systems, and lots of details. If I was communicating with clarity types, I would give them precise details and check in to make sure they are following my logic. You can find a lot of clarity types in accounting and the IT departments.

Identifying the audience's style and being able to switch to that style quickly will undoubtedly improve the effectiveness of the communication. We want to empower the dialogue in an effective way as well. Usually, we communicate our wants and needs or receive the other person's wants and needs. These are generally called expectations. Expectations are, in general, an agreement, an understanding, or, in some cases, a promise.

In a career environment, expectations will be around when we work, where we work, how we work, and what we deliver for work. Deadlines for a project are clear expectations that some work needs to be done by that deadline. Communicating the deadline is setting the expectation. I learned to become more aware of expectations, and if I saw there wasn't a clear expectation, I needed to ask for clarification of what was expected.

I also learned to look for nonverbal expectations. These are more difficult to uncover because they generally involve assumptions. I started to ask myself what assumptions were being made in this situation. This helped me flush out possible expectations. To communicate effectively, I have found that telling people my assumptions and learning their assumptions helps to set realistic expectations.

One way that I found very effective with expectations was to send out an email to list any takeaways, deadlines, or expected work activity. This helped everyone see the expectations and have an opportunity to correct any miscommunicated details. If no feedback was received for correction, then everyone was accepting what to expect from the email. I found this little act of following up on meetings with an email improved my effectiveness of communicating, which increased the likelihood of my project and collaborative work being more successful.

The last key that I worked on was huge, and it took a while to see the effects of believing in myself. Even today, I continue to work on my beliefs. It's like hiking in the Rocky Mountains. Once one summit is reached, the view is magnificent, but it also shows you another much higher peak to climb.

A mentor recently asked me if I understood how the mind worked. I hesitated to answer. The reason is because I know that our minds are very powerful. There are many wonderful mysteries about the mind that we are still exploring. I understand that we have a conscious and subconscious level in our minds. These are very powerful components of our minds.

A lot of our beliefs can easily be identified in our conscious mind. Awareness of those beliefs makes it easier to work on beliefs that hold us back. By working on the beliefs that hold us back, we can reframe, reprogram, or shift our thinking to change the belief to a more empowering way of thinking. It's the beliefs in our subconscious mind that hold us back, or in many cases sabotage our success, that are hard to work on.

The beliefs in our subconscious mind are formed from past events or stories we told ourselves while growing up and learning about different things like money, politics, or different situations. Our minds will work hard to protect us from danger. This protection will arrive at the right time to derail a plan and keep us from living to our full potential. These situations make us wonder why we can't get ahead or fail to succeed. We know what we want but fall short of reaching the goal.

Journaling about a situation is a great way to bring beliefs to the conscious mind. Journaling and analyzing written thoughts can help identify beliefs and how they hold us back. Another great tool is to work with a professional coach who knows how to bring light to these subconscious beliefs. Often, a coach can recognize when a repressed belief comes up in a session and can help work through the belief.

In many situations as a consultant, I have experienced the feeling of Imposter's Syndrome. For me, I felt like I didn't know enough to be consulting. I was afraid someone was going to call me out. In consulting, I was often presented as an expert and a senior resource. In a lot of those situations, I was on a huge project. I had to work on this belief and the stories I was telling myself.

Writing affirmations is a great tool to redirect beliefs. I repeat my affirmations multiple times daily to replace the old beliefs with new ones. I also kept a journal of my achievements and successes. I would review my achievements in the journal regularly to see how much I have experienced and how far I have moved out of my comfort zone. Affirmations and success journals are amazing steps for success in forming new beliefs.

I found that taking small steps more aligned with new beliefs increased the speed of replacing the older non-serving belief. I look for situations where I can take small risks. When those risks worked out in my favor, I would celebrate the success and add it to my success journal.

If, for some reason, the risk was a failure, I would look for a lesson to learn and celebrate that I didn't hold myself back. I had a mentor tell me to get used to failing, and this was failing forward. This helped me reframe failure and not be afraid of taking risks toward an idea or a goal.

Taking small risks will accelerate your successes and lock in your new beliefs. Once I started to use affirmations, journalling, and learning to fail forward with small risks, I saw doors opening, new conversations, and opportunities to break into the management level.

This change didn't happen overnight; I needed consistency with my activities. I had to perform these new practices daily. The days turned into months and then years, and success started to come. Some studies say adapting to a new habit takes about 21 days. In some studies, it is reported it takes closer to 90 days. I think this discrepancy depends on the person, the situation, and how deep the beliefs are. Being more persistent in making the change will be challenging. The more consistent with the process one can be, the better.

In some situations, I could quickly adapt to change and move forward with my beliefs and actions. My communication became more effective when I started to be more deliberate with expectations and knowing how to communicate with others in their style. I also started to behave and function like other managers. Combining all three of these tactics helped me in my career. I went from an individual contributor to a global program manager in a few years. When I hit the program management summit, I saw there were other mountain peaks to climb. I continued to work on my beliefs and take risks out of my comfort zone, which led me to become a manager of a customer care department for a consulting company and quickly moved into a delivery director of an international consulting firm.

I found using modeling, developing an effective communication strategy, and working on my beliefs were the keys to my success in becoming a manager. These three areas are a great place to start for anyone who wants to break a career barrier. An exceptional career path will become a reality for you as it did for me.

***

To contact Steve:

eMail: swalsh@2bexceptional.com

Website: www.2bexceptional.com

LinkedIn: https://www.linkedin.com/in/walshsteve/

Phillip Suggs

Phillip Suggs brings with him over two decades of sales experience in both the Industrial Maintenance Repair Operations and Consumer Package Goods industry. Currently, Phillip is a Performance Capabilities Leader at The Sazerac Company. Prior to his journey into the alcohol beverage space, he worked for Pepsi Beverage Corporation as a Key Account Manager (KAM) for the state of Florida where he consistently drove bottom line results becoming the #1 KAM in the Southeast Division. Over the years, Phillip has developed a skill for connecting the dots between everyday tactics and execution to revenue growth and bottom-line performance. His ability to simplify concepts and strategic agendas has created a passion for becoming a people leader and more importantly developing other professionals. As a former athlete he is determined, competitive and has great people skills that thrive in a team environment.

Phillip is a graduate of Sewanee, The University of the South where he received a Bachelors in Spanish Literature. He later earned his Master's in Business Administration from Florida International University. In the spirit of personal development, during the Covid shutdown, Phillip completed the Lean and Agile Practices Certificate program at Georgetown University along with his Master's in Project Management.

Pandora's Box A Guide to Consumer-Centric Selling
By Phillip Suggs

The legend of Pandora's Box, a cornerstone of ancient Greek mythology, has been recounted through the ages not merely as a tale of curiosity and unintended consequences, but as a profound parable embodying the good and evil of the human experience. According to myth, Pandora, sculpted from the Earth and watered by the divine, was the first woman on the planet and was endowed with gifts by the gods. Among these was a mysterious box accompanied by a singular directive that Pandora must not open it.

Driven by an innate curiosity; a trait that Pandora embodies, reflecting the curious spirit inherent in all humanity, she eventually succumbs to temptation, and opens the box. In doing so, she releases into the world all types of tragedy and misery previously unknown to mankind: disease, despair, malice, and strife scattered about, casting a shadow over the human condition. However, the story holds within it a glimmer of redemption; for after the cascade of calamities, what remains in the box, lying quietly in its corner, is Hope; a powerful symbol indicating that no matter the darkness, light persists.

This ancient narrative finds a surprising parallel in the modern practice of consumer-centric selling, a revolutionary approach in the domain of sales and client relations. Traditional sales methodologies, much like Pandora's initial interaction with the box, have often focused on the surface — the immediate transaction, the product to be sold, devoid of a deeper understanding or connection. They hinge on the assumption that the seller knows best, pushing products without delving into the unique needs or challenges faced by the client.

Consumer-centric selling, however, represents a significant shift from this product-centric approach to one that is profoundly consumer focused. It champions the philosophy of understanding before advising, and of listening before speaking. Sales professionals adopting this approach do not simply present a pre-packaged solution; instead, they embark on a journey with their clients, engaging in a deeper understanding into the 'Pandora's Box' of their unique circumstances, needs, and challenges. This is not an act of unleashing chaos but rather a deliberate process of discovery, aimed at bringing to light not obstacles but opportunities for solutions, collaboration, and mutual benefit.

By drawing parallels between the unfolding chaos from Pandora's Box and the exploratory process inherent in consumer-centric selling, we find a compelling framework for understanding the transformative power of empathy, listening, and genuine engagement in sales. Just as Pandora's act led to the emergence of troubles followed by the revelation of hope, the consumer-centric approach involves navigating through the complexities and challenges of the client's world to ultimately uncover solutions; the 'hope' within the box.

This approach demands a re-evaluation of what it means to be a sales professional. It's about transitioning from the role of a vendor to that of a trusted advisor, one who understands that before the 'evils', the challenges and obstacles faced by the client can be addressed, they must first be understood. In this light, a sales professional's role becomes akin to that of Pandora after the chaos. A bearer of hope, armed not with a product, but with the promise of solutions tailored to the client's deepest needs and concerns.

In this expanded introduction, we delve into the rich symbolism of Pandora's Box and its relevance to modern consumer-centric selling. By understanding this mythology and its connection to contemporary sales practices, professionals can gain profound insights into the importance of consumer-centricity. Ultimately, the legend teaches us that to truly assist a client, one must first thoroughly understand them, their issues, concerns, and pain points. Just as Pandora's Box is more than just a tale of misfortune, consumer-centric selling is more than just a method; it's a journey towards understanding, collaboration, and, ultimately, hope.

The story of Pandora teaches us that with every challenge comes opportunity. In the world of a sales professional, each client's needs and problems represent the "evils" that escaped Pandora's Box but hidden among these challenges is the opportunity to provide genuine help and solutions — the hope that remained in the box.

Basics of Consultative Selling: Principles and Practices

Sales professionals, much like the mythological Pandora, are introduced to navigating the complex landscape of sales. However, this story marks a departure from ancient tragedy to modern enlightenment, illustrating the essence of consumer-centric selling. This approach in sales, contrasted with Pandora's unwitting release of chaos, champions a deliberate and introspective exploration into the client's world.

Client Understanding

A sales professional's transformation begins with a critical realization: that true understanding transcends superficial interactions. Much like Pandora's box, each client holds a repository of unseen challenges and underlying desires, obscured by the facade of expressed needs or immediate concerns. A sales professional's journey into consumer-centric selling is marked by their shift in perspective — from a focus on the external to an in-depth exploration of the internal landscapes of their clients.

This profound change in approach requires an individual to harness their curiosity constructively. It starts with an approach to each client interaction with the mindset of an explorer, seeking to understand the hidden layers beneath the surface. This is not merely curiosity but a strategic, empathetic, and patient inquiry into the client's world. As a result, a sales professional will learn to recognize that every client's needs are as unique as the myriad of evils Pandora unwittingly unleashed, yet within them lie opportunities for growth, connection, and resolution.

Active Listening and Probing Questions

This evolution in the sales realm is also characterized by a commitment to active listening, which is a cornerstone of the consumer-centric selling approach. What we learn by listening, truly listening, involves more than just hearing words; it is about understanding context, sensing unspoken concerns, and acknowledging the emotional undercurrents of the client's narrative. This level of attentiveness allows sales professionals to ask more meaningful, probing questions that cut to the heart of the client's issues, much like carefully peeling away the layers of an onion to reveal the core.

This transition from a product-centric to a client-centric mindset mirrors the moment Pandora opens the box — except, in the case of a consumer-centric sales professional, each revelation is handled with care, intention, and a focus on resolution. Their inquiries are not mere formalities but genuine attempts to understand and empathize with the client's situation, analogous to gently lifting the lid of Pandora's box, mindful of the consequences and focused on uncovering the hidden hope within.

Empathy, Needs Assessment, and Customized Solutions

The crux of a consumer-centric selling approach lies in empathy: the ability to feel and understand the client's situation as if it were your own. This empathetic approach propels professionals to conduct a thorough needs assessment, probing into the client's objectives, challenges, and the context in which they operate. Just as Pandora's box contained complexities beyond initial appearances, we discover that each client's needs encompass layers of intricacy and nuance.

Armed with a deeper understanding, Sales professionals become adept at crafting customized solutions — strategies and recommendations tailored specifically to the unique contours of each client's situation. This made-to-measure approach contrasts starkly with the one-size-fits-all solutions of traditional sales tactics. It's about finding the unique 'hope' within each 'box' — developing answers that genuinely address the client's individual challenges and aspirations.

The Path Forward: From Despair to Hope

As sales professionals continue to refine their approach, their interactions become more meaningful, their solutions become more impactful. They find that by embracing the principles of consumer-centricity, empathy, deep understanding, and personalized solutions can transform potential client despair into hope. This is the intrinsic nature of a sales professional's distinction from Pandora: where her curiosity released chaos, a consumer-centric sales professional's careful, empathetic exploration fosters clarity and resolution.

In adopting these practices, professionals not only elevate their relationships, but also redefine their own role within them. This transitions sales professionals from being seen as a typical peddler to being valued as a trusted advisor, consultant, and partner in solving problems rather than just a source of products. This transformative journey from selling to solving, from telling to listening, and from assuming to understanding, encapsulates the foundational principles and practices of consumer-centric selling.

This should serve as a parable for sales professionals navigating the modern market. It offers a map for navigating the complexities of human needs and desires, urging a shift from fleeting transactional interactions to meaningful connections, and highlighting the transformative power of understanding, empathy, and tailored solutions in the realm of sales.

Real-life Application

So, you may be asking yourself, "How does all of this work in real life?" In theory, this all sounds great, but practical application is necessary to be successful as a consumer-centric sales professional. Here is a real example that I personally experienced while working for one of the largest beverage companies in the world.

It was a Tuesday morning around eight. John, who was one of my top team members, says, "Hey Phil, I am at the Walmart over in Westchester, Miami, and Miguel, the store manager, does not want the 2-liter deal that is on ad this week." My immediate response was, "That doesn't make any sense. What do you mean he doesn't want the deal? The Fourth of July is this Saturday." John says, "I know, but he doesn't want the deal." At this point, I genuinely still couldn't fathom why Miguel, whom we have an established relationship with, is not taking in this deal. I told John, my sales rep, to stay at the store and that I was on my way.

Now, before I go any further, let me provide some context. In the beverage industry, during the summer, from mid-May through the end of August, we refer to it as the "100 Days of Summer." It is important to know that during this time, our company would generate more volume and revenue in these 100 days than the rest of the year. Let me say that again. We would generate more volume and revenue in 100 days than we did in the other 265 days of the year. Not to mention, this particular store was in the heart of Miami, which is one of the hottest places on Earth during the summer months. And to top it all off, the Fourth of July fell on a Saturday this year. I imagine you can understand why I was bewildered that we were not executing this promo deal.

So, I get to the store, and I immediately see John, and I am like, "Help me understand what the problem is," because this just doesn't make sense. At this point, we see Miguel, the store manager, come around the corner, and I say, "Miguel, what's up? John tells me you don't want the 2-liter deal, and I am trying to understand why." He then asked me how we were going to execute the display, and I told him that it would come in 60 cases on a four-by-four-foot pallet with base wrap.

For those of you who are not familiar with how 2-liter carbonated soft drinks are packaged, they come 8 bottles to a case, ten cases to a layer, stacked six layers high. When I mentioned to Miguel that we were asking for a full pallet, he immediately shot it down. As a seasoned sales professional, my curiosity kicked in. I simply asked Miguel why he was against the pallet execution, and his response to me was, "I don't like the mess it leaves behind." His concern was that when the consumers shop the pallet display, the plastic shells that are left behind would leave a mess. After confirming the issue, I thought I had an immediate solution. So, I offered to send a merchandiser every two hours to maintain the display. Oddly enough, Miguel says, "Yeah, I don't think so." Even assuring him that I would have someone on call, he still wouldn't go for it. At this point, I am at a loss, and Miguel can tell that I am in disbelief that he is passing up the potential revenue driver that this promo would provide. Then Miguel says this, "God forbid this display becomes a mess and someone trips over one of the plastic crates, hurts themselves, and decides to sue the store." Out of curiosity, I asked him who would cover the litigation cost in that type of situation, and he informed me that it comes out of the store's P&L. That, in turn, would affect the store's performance and ultimately his bonus.

At this point, I knew what the real issue was and how to solve it, but I wanted to make sure that was the only issue. So, I confirmed that the issue was not the promo deal, not the pallet execution, and not even the potential mess. In fact, it was the potential to be sued by a consumer that would put a strain on the store P&L, affecting the store's performance, and ultimately affecting the potential bonus payout. As I mentioned earlier, from previous interactions, through trust and rapport, we had developed a great relationship with Miguel. So I was able to empathize with his concern because, in the end, this could affect his livelihood. So, I said to Miguel, "Would you take the deal if I can execute the promo without the pallet and the potential mess with the 2-liter crates?" He responded, "Can you do that" and I said, "I have a rack that can hold the 60 cases without the plastic crates." As a sales professional, by taking a consumer-centric approach, you may find yourself going down what seems like a path of chaos that eventually leads you to the real problem and ultimately a valued solution. In the end, not only did we execute the deal, but instead of executing 60 cases we executed 240 cases, which was four times larger than the original ask. Always remember, when you solve the problem, you make the sale.

Embracing Chaos, A Call to Action

In the dynamic landscape of sales, embracing a consumer approach can transform challenges into opportunities for growth and success. This method revolves around a deeper, consumer-centric engagement, moving beyond transactions to forge meaningful relationships and deliver tailored solutions. Here's how sales professionals can embrace chaos and uncover solutions through a consultative selling strategy.

Understanding the Consultative Approach

Consultative selling is fundamentally about understanding the client's needs, concerns, and the context in which they operate. Unlike traditional sales methods focused on quick transactions, this approach requires a deep dive into the client's world, similar to opening a metaphorical 'box' of their entire business. The aim is to uncover hidden challenges and unarticulated needs, which often lie beneath the surface of initial conversations. By taking a deep dive into Miguel's world and opening his metaphorical box we were able to peel back his layers of concern.

Navigating Uncertainty with Curiosity

When I received the initial phone call from John, the store sales rep, I was curious. It was this curiosity that triggered the inclination to truly understand Miguel's main concern. Today, businesses are more complex than ever, and experience constant change. Sales professionals today are faced with what can be described as chaos with a myriad of unknowns and ambiguity that vary depending on each client's situation. Navigating this chaos starts with curiosity. By adopting a mindset of exploration and inquiry, sales professionals can transform uncertainty into a path of discovery. This involves asking open-ended questions, actively listening, and seeking to understand the client's perspective without preconceived notions.

Achieving Clarity through Understanding

The ability to ask open ended questions, and probe for clarity, sometimes referred to as 'root cause analysis, allowed us to get to the real issue. The ability to peel back each layer of concern was like opening a door to the core of why we were getting a "no." The next step was to put together the information gathered through active listening and empathy into a meaningful understanding of the client's needs by identifying not only the explicit but also the implicit challenges Miguel faced.

Transforming Challenges into Opportunities

The challenge that my team member and I faced that day was an opportunity in disguise. The essence of consultative selling lies in using the insights gained through empathy and understanding to address client challenges in a way that adds genuine value. Instead of fearing the 'evils'; the countless problems clients may present. Sales professionals should view them as opportunities to demonstrate their understanding, expertise, and commitment to the client's success. Each solution should be framed as an answer to a specific challenge, tailored to the client's unique concerns and goals. The insights we gained by understanding Miguel's needs led to providing a solution that created both functional and emotional value.

Building Relationships through Empathy

When clients are incentivized by performance, metrics become a major appeal point for them. Understanding and empathizing with Miguel's concern for costly litigations created trust and rapport that reinforced our credibility and fostered a positive relationship. Empathy is central to the consultative approach. It allows sales professionals to connect with clients on a human level, fostering trust and openness. By genuinely understanding Miguel's point of view and feeling his challenges as if they were our own, we were able to reinforce our rapport and foundation for a long-term relationship. This relationship was crucial when devising solutions that genuinely addressed his concerns and aspirations.

The consultative approach transforms the nature of the relationship between clients and sales professionals. By moving away from transactional interactions and towards a partnership model, where sales professionals position themselves as trusted advisors, you become invaluable to your clients. This shift not only enhances client satisfaction but also leads to more sustainable and fruitful business outcomes.

A Call to Action for Sales Professionals

Embracing the chaos inherent in all client's needs and market conditions requires a shift from traditional sales tactics to a consultative, client-centric approach. Sales professionals should be encouraged to cultivate curiosity, empathy, and a deep understanding of their clients. By doing so, we can transform sales interactions from mere transactions to meaningful exchanges that deliver real value and foster long-term relationships. This approach not only elevates the sales profession but also ensures that clients receive the thoughtful, personalized solutions they need. In the ever-evolving world of sales, the ability to navigate complexity and chaos with a consumer-centric mindset will be the hallmark of success.

Cracking The Rich Code: The True Meaning of Riches

As a sales professional, I often hear people say, "I could never be in sales", and they then go on to say things like, "I don't like to ask for people's money," or "I am afraid of being told no." What many people fail to realize is that we are all in sales. Whether you are a toddler asking your parents for candy, a teenager trying to campaign to your parents to buy you a car or sitting in an interview convincing an employer to hire you, it's all sales. In your journey towards "Cracking the Rich Code," the adoption of a consumer-centric selling approach is a pivotal framework for amassing not just riches, but lasting value and relevance in the market. This approach, rooted in understanding, empathy, and genuine problem-solving, transforms not just sales professionals, but any individual from a mere vendor to an indispensable partner. By focusing on providing true value to the end user, a sales professional becomes invaluable, embodying the very essence of being indispensable. This shift in approach does not purely aim at immediate gains but fosters long-term relationships, trust, and loyalty, setting a foundation for sustainable success. Hence, in the pursuit of riches, the paradox becomes clear: by prioritizing the value we bring to others above the wealth we seek for ourselves, we unlock a more profound, enduring form of wealth. In this light, "Cracking the Rich Code" through consumer-centric selling reveals that when you focus on making yourself valuable to others, the riches you seek will invariably find you, redefining the very concept of success in the realm of sales and beyond.

Let this serve as a reminder: the path to becoming rich, in all the forms that truly matter, is paved with curiosity, empathy, and the relentless pursuit of solutions. As you turn the pages of this book and reflect on your own journey, consider the value you bring to the world. It is in this value, in the problems you solve for others, that you may find the greatest riches of all.

***

To contact Phillip:

E: pfsuggs3@me.com

C: (786) 518-0560

Cecelia "Fi" Mazanke

Cecelia "Fi" Mazanke is the Founder and CEO of Direct Connect Coaching. Fi's formal training as an Executive Leadership Coaching began in 1998. Fi received three levels of certification as part of her coaching training, including Mastery Level Certification. Fi blazed a trail in 1999 when she introduced coaching into her company after being a sales promotion manager there for 12 years. Within the first year as a coach, Fi and her clients saw transformational results. After a year and a half of coaching there, Fi decided to diversify her client profile, left her corporate coaching role, and began Direct Connect Coaching. Soon, Fi saw the emergence of a diverse client niche in her coaching practice.

Fi's work as an Executive Leadership Coach grew as organizations began to hire her for their corporate results. Executives from across the globe saw the value of the simple yet effective tools that she uses to generate results from sales, recruiting, marketing, and innovative ideas in customer success and sales operations.

Her passion is to empower those in an influential role to lead from their heart space. "In today's work environment, leaders are looking to influence their teams to do their best work. That influence comes when the leader is feeling a sense of calm confidence within themselves," states Fi. Fi coaches leaders and teams to support them in remembering how to be connected to their own visions and, most importantly, to connect to their hearts as a guiding light.

The World's Richest Shoeshine Man

By Cecelia Mazanke

Most people define richness by the amount of money in their bank accounts. While money can offer the freedom of time and exceptional resources that you have access to, we can consider expanding the definition so that you can feel a sense of richness in your own life.

In 1996, I was at a conference at a very luxurious hotel in Phoenix. I have always been an early riser, and this day was no exception. I took the elevator down to the lobby to find a cup of coffee. At a station adjacent to the front desk sat a shoeshine man. He was a tall, thin black man who was there to shine the hotel guests' shoes. I remember him vividly in my mind because he graciously greeted me as I disembarked the elevator. He was the happiest man I ever met. After a lovely conversation with him, I went about my search for coffee. This man, I cannot remember his name, joyfully sang in the hotel's lobby and greeted his customers with equal fervor. He impacted my life so much that I can still picture him and smile at the very thought of him nearly thirty years later. Each morning, I went down to the lobby and was met with more enthusiasm than the day prior. That meaningful encounter with "The Happiest Shoeshine Man" impacted me deeply. I thought to myself, "If this man can be that happy shining shoes, I can be happy in my then career as a Sales Promotion Manager." In fact, I was quite certain that I was earning a much higher income than he was; however, you would not know it based on his overall attitude of shining shoes.

So, my shoeshine man helped me to reframe my definition of rich. He demonstrated to me how happiness and being an interested, gleeful human being made him rich. To greet each day with such powerful energy and vitality would be something that I would aspire to in my own life.

Now, nearly 30 years later, I would have more clarity on the steps to achieving what my mentor, Mary Morrissey, calls Full Spectrum Wealth. Full Spectrum Wealth is something that I work with my clients to achieve. I've been an Executive Leadership Coach for the past 25 years. I've had the honor of bringing these empowering principles to my clients to create financial wealth, impact their physical and mental health and their relationships, and generate work that makes their hearts sing.

Several foundational principles formulate the basis for creating well-rounded richness. Experiencing an abundant life is an inside-out job. All results that we see on the outside begin with this foundational concept. Results are created from the thoughts we think, which leads to our emotions. Emotions lead to action steps (or inaction if we are stuck), and this leads to the results we see in our outer world. When people understand that they are not victims in this world but rather creators, the doors are open to infinite possibilities.

Let's begin with a clear understanding of two critical components directly impacting your ability to create wealth. I have successfully used these principles in my coaching practice for the past 25 years and have had the joy of witnessing remarkable and sometimes miraculous transformations with my clients. The first principle is called The Emotional Discovery Process. This proprietary process I have developed uses the body's wisdom to unearth roadblocks of fears that prevent success. Many years ago, I learned from Dr. Martin Plotkin that the body always tells the truth. Most people, however, look to the mind for the truth. When we clearly understand that our body contains a truth meter on the inside, we can rely on the physical sensations within the body to know what decisions are best for us. How do you do that? Well, you simply hold the decision that you are looking to make in your mind. When the mind holds a specific scenario, that scenario will elicit a physical feeling sensation within the body. If the physical feeling is expansive, that indicates a YES for you. Suppose the physical scenario creates a restrictive feeling within the body, that indicates a NO for you. I have used this formula of using the body's wisdom to discern what is best for my clients, specifically when making decisions with job offers or even new hires. I share with my clients that sometimes a person's resume does not always give you the best indication of a great fit for your team. Using the body's wisdom is a more effective tool in using your internal guidance system to determine what is best for you.

After a client clearly understands how to use the body's wisdom to discern what is best, we look to clear any roadblocks of fear that may be preventing the client's success. You see, under normal circumstances, a client's neuropeptides, which are a group of compounds that act as neurotransmitters, flow easily throughout the body. When a client experiences a trauma, then the neuropeptides do not flow normally, and then an emotion is stuck in cellular memory. Often, the client is unaware that the cellular memory exists in his/her body. It is an unconscious roadblock. Our natural state is love, so when fear is held in the body's cellular memory, a client might be held back from experiencing the desired success. By coaching thousands of people over these past 25 years, I have learned that when a client tells me what he is struggling with currently, that current struggle stems from a cellular memory that is anchored in some form of fear.

In the Emotional Discovery Process, I take my clients through a closed-eye visualization, which allows them to fully feel the "stuck emotion." Then, the client, through their body's wisdom, can experience the timing of when that emotion got stuck in her body. Once we find said emotion, the process acts like pulling the weed out from the root. The client can see the association between the difficulty they are currently experiencing and the stored emotion from her past. I call this an Associated Emotion. Once the client feels the connection between the two emotions, we can move the client into forgiveness of the experience, which moves the client from fear to love, his natural state. Then, voila! Forgiveness becomes the healing balm necessary for the client to feel better. The client also has a much greater reduction or complete elimination of the charge from that stuck emotion and can generate results she loves.

Since money or lack of money can have cellular memory experiences associated with it, the process of eliminating the cause of stress around lack of money is a very effective tool for creating wealth and healthy money habits. One client I worked with years ago amassed a debt to the Internal Revenue Service. His debt totaled well over $100,000. He came to me with this very stressful situation looming, and it was impacting his marriage and his business results. We were able to pull the money weeds out by the roots, and almost immediately, he devised a plan to pay off his debt. We created a clear vision of what he was experiencing and feeling when the debt was paid in full. He and his wife would celebrate the debt being cleared in one year, and they would enjoy a delicious meal at their favorite restaurant and toast their freedom from debt. Well, James did just that, and a year later, I received his text that he had made his final payment to the IRS, and he and his wife were happily celebrating what appeared to be a problem that would take years to solve.

After we use the Emotional Discovery Process to move into connection to love, we then move to the Design Process. The Design Process is an effective tool that answers the question, "What would I love?" in these four areas of one's life: health and well-being, relationships, vocation (work), and time and money freedom. In the Design Process, the client becomes the architect of her vision and crafts her dream life. We use the question, "What would I love? "Rather than what are my goals, because love is the highest frequency that we are. When you answer, "What would I love?" you are constructing the dream you have for your life. When you design your vision in the four quadrants, you write it as if it is in the present tense. Then, you bring pictures to your imagination as if you are living that dream life right now. Those pictures create a feeling sensation in your body and remember the neurotransmitters we mentioned in the Emotional Discovery Process; those neurotransmitters are activated by the parasympathetic nervous system. The neurotransmitters send a signal to the universe that acts as if you are already experiencing the life of your dreams. In this very expansive body space, out of the blue, things start to show up in your life.

An example of this happened with a recent client. We worked through many of his financial roadblocks. He decided to go one day with a patient of his to a tattoo conference. His patient had a detailed tattoo, which took three hours to complete. As a result of the long wait, the person after his patient, canceled on the tattoo artist. The patient said that only leaves room for one person to get tattooed. That person was my client, whom he called Doc. He said Doc, it's time for you to get your tattoo. To incentivize my client, his patient said that he would pay the first $50 of the tattoo. Normally, the intricacies of a tattoo my client wanted would cost thousands of dollars. The tattoo artist got to work and never agreed to a price. So, once he was finished, the tattoo artist said they never discussed pricing. The artist said let's agree upon $200 for the tattoo. With his patient paying $50, the remaining balance for his tattoo was $150. My client shared with me that he never really carries cash with him, but he decided to get cash for the conference. He could not believe his eyes when he realized that he had exactly $150 in his wallet to pay for this tattoo, which normally would have cost thousands. These are some of the remarkable stories that happen when you remove your limiting beliefs and lack of mentality around money and all other areas of your life.

Years ago, I worked with an executive named Kathy. Kathy lost both her mother and her father in a period of 6 months. Once we cleared the roadblocks of Kathy's grief through my proprietary process, called the Emotional Discovery Process, we were able to get busy with designing Kathy's business success. We created a vision of what she would love her business to look like. She got very clear, using the Law of Specificity, and detailed the number of team members she had on her team and the characteristics of her team, what business traits the team portrayed, and even had a crystal-clear vision of how they would be celebrating their success together.

Eager to transform from a flailing business manager to a thriving business leader, Kathy got very serious about rehearsing her vision daily, acting as if her vision was her reality, and taking the inspired action steps to be in service to her vision. Just two years later, Kathy was in a meeting in February, where, in the past, she would make up numbers of team members to report to her peers so as not to look embarrassed at this meeting. During the meeting, I received a text message from Kathy. She shared her team's depth chart, and it was exactly as she planned two years prior when she had a small team with no growth. Here, she realized her vision and had a thriving team of 20 managers. She also realized her dream of becoming a millionaire by the time she was 36. In a short period, Kathy went from a grief-stricken sales manager with no development of future sales leaders to a thriving leader. Kathy was able to let go of what she was lacking in life, including the loss of both of her parents, within a 6-month time frame to create results in her business that grew from 2 to 20 offices.

Kathy demonstrated the power of her ability to move from her conditions, circumstances, and problems to a life that she loved living. She even used her vision and the Emotional Discovery Process to welcome 2 beautiful baby girls into the world. Kathy's birth of both of her daughters amazed the nurses, as she had calm, peaceful, and pain-free births. I am happy to share with you that Kathy is living a rich life and is now bringing some of these tools that she learned in her business to the teachers in her daughter's school.

Let us take a quick review of how Kathy transformed her life from one that was sad and lacking into one that was rich and blessed with what she loved.

1. Kathy let go of low-frequency feelings of grief by feeling those emotions in her body and forgiving what she felt she wanted to forgive.

2. Kathy generated a vision that felt aligned with her definition of success. She described that vision with specific details about what her team would look like and accomplish in it.

3. Kathy rehearsed her vision daily with feeling and as if it was her reality.

4. Kathy took inspired action steps in service to her vision.

Over the years, I have also used gratitude in my own life and in my clients' lives to directly connect them to abundance. I have learned that there are different levels of gratitude. When we first learn about gratitude, we are grateful FOR something or someone. We receive a gift, and we send a thank you card. As we grow, we can learn to become grateful in advance of something. When we are grateful in advance, we create the expectation of receiving what we are grateful for, even though we do not see it yet. This concept of being grateful in advance has also helped my clients to understand that we can use gratitude as a connection to a higher mindset. Gratitude allows us to access new thoughts, ideas, and solutions instead of remaining stuck in problem-based thinking.

How can you use gratitude to your advantage to generate more wealth? First, check in with yourself. Do you focus your thoughts on what you are lacking? Lack thoughts lead to lack feelings, which leads to lack results. You will always know what you are focusing on simply by feeling what is going on inside your body. When you feel an expansion inside your body, you are connected to abundance-based thoughts. When you feel restrictions in your body, you are connected to lack or limiting thoughts. It's that simple. So, how can you bring greater awareness to noticing what you are noticing inside your body?

What does it take to create a million-dollar business in a year? My client, Niles, chose to work with me in early 2022 with that challenge. He was far from this daunting feat, and year after year, he fell far short of achieving a million dollars in sales in his office. I asked Niles if he was willing to use unconventional methods to achieve this dream and receive the abundant income that came with this achievement. Niles was ready. We went straight to work. He was willing to release any of his limiting beliefs in his million-dollar dream through The Emotional Discovery Process. Next, Niles and I created his very detailed vision of his Million Dollar Dream. It included where he was and what he and his team did to celebrate this vision being his reality. It took until the final week of December, and I am happy to say that Niles did it and texted me the wonderful news of his dream coming true.

You have access to an infinite number of possibilities in Cracking the Rich Code. The key to it all is that the power to crack your own personal rich code lies within you. All the answers to your questions about living your best life start from the inside out. Many people look for solutions outside of themselves. However, when you get crystal clear about the things that bring you life and you focus your energy on those things, you have the ability to serve others with your God-given gifts and talents. In that service, there is a sense of fulfillment unknown to the common man. The example of you living a life that you absolutely love becomes your greatest asset and provides you with riches that cannot be measured but rather felt by you and those who witness you living such a beautiful and abundantly blessed life.

May you use these tools to live a rich life that you absolutely love!

***

To contact Cecelia:

For additional information on individual or team coaching, go to our website at directconnectcoaching.co or e-mail Fi directly at fimazanke@gmail.com.

Jim Diebold

Having been both an on-the-road sales leader and a small business owner, Jim Diebold knows what it is like working sixty hours a week. Jim knows how easy it is to be drawn to tasks that keep you working IN your business instead of ON your business. He has also lived the scenario of coming home after those long days spent at the office or traveling and feeling distant from the family. He was either missing his son's functions or not being fully present at home.

Jim became a certified FocalPoint Executive Coach and Trainer because, after twenty years in the corporate and business ownership spaces, he needed to work in a more impactful role for the people he was serving. So now he works as a silent partner, a confidant, walking hand-in-hand with business owners and team leaders, helping solve the challenges around time, talent, and growth. The businesses scale faster than thought possible and the owner/leader get their time back.

Jim is an award-winning FocalPoint coach and is participating in his second collaboration with *Cracking the Rich Code*. Jim has been married to his amazing bride, Cindy, for twenty-nine years. They have a son, Jack. They love all things outdoors, especially enjoying an early cup of coffee by the firepit.

How Effective is Your Sales Process
By Jim Diebold

In my experience, most organizations do not have a formal sales process. If they do have one, most of the time it is not formally written anywhere. There seems to be an underlying theme that when a salesperson is hired, all that needs to be done is teach them about the product(s) or service(s), send them on their way, and wait for the orders to come rolling in. There may be a weekly, or monthly, meeting to ascertain what projects are expected to be entered for the month, but no significant training is provided during these meetings. Just a quick status check to report up the ladder and then send everyone back out to the streets.

Have you ever watched a professional baseball player have a bad at-bat or make a bad play in the field? If the camera is on them as they enter the dugout, what do you see? They have a consultation with one of the coaches; this could be the hitting coach or bench coach for perspective. Why does this happen? Because despite the fact that they're professionals, they still need assistance. Of course, there are expectations to perform at that level. Their skills were deemed acceptable at the "interview." But that does not mean they can join any team and automatically perform with perfection. We have variables like team members, management, processes, support, and execution that can and will affect the performance of each member.

Before discussing creating a scalable sales process, I want to quickly address training. Athletes train in between games. Salespeople tend to only receive on-the-job training. Imagine a professional team using each game as their training grounds. A few quick stats: According to *taskdrive*, some statistics show that "60% of companies take a random or informal approach to sales training."[1] 69% of salespeople describe themselves as self-taught.[2] And according to *Spotio*, "84% of sales professionals say their sales training is forgotten within three months."[3]

This matters immensely because two of the key components of our sales process are presentation and overcoming objections. How well and how often do you train your team?

Our Sales Process Steps:

Client Prospecting

The first step of our sales process is to identify who our ideal clients are. Some of this responsibility falls into the marketing team's bucket. But if your sales team is required to make cold calls of any kind, they need to be dialing the right numbers or knocking on the right doors. There are some key factors that need to be determined before sending the sales team out prospecting.

Here are some questions that need consideration when you're determining clients:

- What do we really sell?
- What solution does the product/service provide?
- Who actually needs this product? Is it manufacturing facilities of a certain size or geography? Urgent care or surgical facilities?
- Are they ready to purchase *now*? ('now' meaning within a reasonable sales cycle time for your product or service). Too often salespeople get strung along by the account that says they are interested in the product, but there is always a reason why there are delays in moving forward. This is a big time-suck, and it starts to look really bad when that account(s) is still on your call report as 'almost ready to buy'.

The more specific an organization becomes around who their ideal client is, the easier it is for a salesperson to take a rifle approach in their prospecting efforts. Obtaining a meeting can be hard enough on its own. Don't set the team up for failure by not having a specific definition as to who the organization's ideal client is. At this time, it also makes sense to know who your competitors are and what your unique selling proposition is. This information will help in our next couple of steps.

Qualifying Leads

This may be done with a short phone call or maybe even an in-person meeting. Here our goal is to build rapport; we need to build a relationship. For the salesperson, you must do research on the organization you're meeting. They most certainly have on you. It goes a long way when you understand their organization and/or industry. You don't have to be an expert. You just need enough information to be able to ask great questions or make great comments. One way to get your prospect talking is to ask them, "What do you know/what have you heard about [MY COMPANY]?" This approach can be a great ice breaker. Another bolder question is, "Why us? Why now?" This is more direct but will give you a key insight as to why they took the meeting.

Between a good mix of personal and business questions, we can determine if this prospect is a good fit for our product or service and company. Which blends right into the next step.

Identifying Needs

As the conversation continues, asking great questions allows us to identify their need(s).

Early in my career, I did not ask very good questions. As a matter of fact, I often asked, "What can I do for you today?" The answer I typically got was, "Nothing". Anyone else relate? As I look back on it, I got that response because my question didn't incite an emotional need. Speaking of not generating need, it is quite common to start providing several features and benefits – facts- to your prospect or client - Snore. If you lead with features and benefits (and then price), then you can lose the account tomorrow to the next person that comes in and does a better job pitching features and benefits and price. The question is, how do you know if those features and benefits are even important to your prospect? We do the same thing to existing clients when we launch a new product or service. We provide the facts. *Telling is not selling!* We have to ask questions. Asking the right questions is imperative to elicit trust and emotion in the process to build a new or maintain an existing relationship.

Our questions need to find out what their challenges are. They need to be open-ended. After asking a question, we need to stop talking and take notes. Here's an important tip: *ask one question at a time.* Don't question stack, which is asking a string of questions in rapid succession. "Steve, are there challenges you are currently having? Is there something that keeps you up at night? If 'it' was no longer a problem, what would 'it' be?" Sound familiar? It's a common habit.

Instead, what if we said something like this, "Steve, I appreciate the time you are giving me right now. I have something I would like to share with you. Before we get to that though, what project is the most pressing for you right now?" Steve answers. Your response, "How does that affect your [time, ability to perform your job, enter whatever phrase makes sense]?" This gets them talking. You are taking notes. They are starting to realize you care and want to work alongside them towards a solution.

My favorite questions to ask are those you already know the answer to. For many of you, you have a product or service that addresses a certain challenge or set of challenges. And because of this, you can ask questions that will start getting you 'yes' responses. Why is that important? Because we want positive words to be used in the conversation ("Yes, I want to buy that"). It also shows you understand their challenges for their industry.

Here's another important tip: *you are just asking questions; you are not talking about your product or service.* "Steve, based on some market research in the XYZ industry, a common challenge is parts don't ship on time. How are you dealing with that?" That is not specifically a 'yes' response question, but it does demonstrate your knowledge around the industry. You could, however, ask it as a closed-ended question to get the 'yes' response. One thing I do want to address is that we are talking about rules here, rather than exceptions. I realize that in some of these examples, your prospect could respond opposite to what you are expecting. That's okay. You just have to be ready to field that response with a follow-up, open-ended question. Keep them talking. Keep taking notes. In these exchanges, the one talking the least is in control of the conversation. Your goal is to lead them to your pool of water and ultimately take a drink. At the end of this chapter, I am going to give you a peek into how you can increase your chances of creating a great exchange with your prospect, and thus increase your chances of closing the sale.

Presentation

So far, we have identified our ideal client, built rapport with our prospect, and uncovered their needs by asking open-ended questions. Step four of our seven-step sales process is the actual presentation. This step is going to have a similar look and feel to uncovering their needs. Now is the opportunity to inject some facts – the features and benefits. But we are also going to ask more questions, many closed-ended and related to information they gave us in the previous step. This step is not necessarily very long. If you have done a great job uncovering their needs, this part can be fairly quick and straightforward. Now we are simply demonstrating that our product or service is the solution.

Think back to guiding your prospect to your pool of water. Well, now it's time to get them to take a drink. By strategically using the information they provided in the last step, you can get them to do so. We want to take an approach called gap selling. Now we understand what their ideal situation looks like as well as where they are now. The in-between space is the gap, and your product or service is the gap filler. "Steve, you shared one of your primary challenges are that parts don't ship on time. This causes delays and equates to $1M of costs per year to fix. While $0 is not likely, you also shared that just a 50% reduction would be considered a huge win." We know their gap from our questions, and we just re-stated it. Why? First, it shows we were paying attention. Second, we want to get the emotional connection going on the pain point they have and the solution you are about to provide. But there is one more piece we can use here to help paint the picture for our prospect – a story. After all, *"facts tell, and stories sell"*.

Using stories helps in multiple ways. Using stories gives validity to your product or service. Not only has someone else experienced what you are offering, but equally important, your prospect is not the only one with this challenge. They aren't alone! The overall concept is to be able to provide some important features and benefits about what you are offering and tie it to what their needs are. This is the best way to demonstrate you have the solution to fill their need.

Objections

Step five of the process can be a lot of fun. Invigorating for you if you have the right mindset. This step of the process is overcoming objections. Gasp! There are many types of objections that may need to be overcome during the course of your presentation. There are also multiple ways to do so. In this segment I want to address the difference between an objection and a condition, one of the most common objections, and one of the best ways to overcome most objections. This step lends itself to having fear set in. Depending on the objection posed, the job done to understand the needs, and the confidence of the salesperson, fear can take hold and derail the process. If we look at objections as a good thing, we can change our attitude towards them. If someone is providing objections, there is interest. They have been paying attention. And that is all we need to know we have an opportunity to continue the conversation.

First, what is the difference between an objection and a condition? In short, an objection can be overcome, whereas a condition cannot. An objection is someone disagreeing with you or maybe challenging you about information you have provided. There is a logical answer to an objection. A condition is an absolute and is a deal stopper. Maybe the facility is closing. Maybe they were acquired by a company that already sells what you sell. You get the idea.

One of, if not, the most common objections is about … price. What's the cost? And this objection can come up at any time in your conversation, or even before the conversation starts! If the first question out of your prospect's mouth is regarding price, you might have an uphill battle. A simple question to retort with is, "How key will the price be in determining moving forward?" Keep them talking. Get more information. If you fall for the trap of the price question, it may be hard or even impossible to get the sale. You have not been able to demonstrate the value of your solution yet. They have not been able to correlate cost and value yet. This is not a position you want to be in.

Of course, price is always going to be a concern. The question is, to what degree? It is highly unlikely that everything in that building is of the least costly items available. And it is likely they have a pride value in the products they are producing. Inside the organization, there is a connection to value. Your questions to overcome their objections have to determine what the most important feature or benefit is of what you offer. Rarely, it is truly the price. Price is used many times as an excuse. If we explore price a little further, when someone says, "That's more than I expected it would cost," is that really an objection? Not really. There is obvious interest. They had formulated value around the product based on what you had done up to that point. Now we just need to explore that comment and solidify our value.

Lastly, what method can we use to overcome many objections? First, let me say you can't use this too many times in the same conversation. It will sound too obvious. But you can change the wording a bit. Second, this approach is powerful because it touches on some emotional triggers: you validate their comment; it lets the prospect know they are not alone in their thoughts; you demonstrate others were satisfied after becoming a client. All of this is accomplished by using three simple words – Feel, Felt, and Found. A response to an objection might look like this, "Steve, I appreciate how you feel. I have other clients that have felt the same way. But after implementing our software, they found the savings were multiple times more than the cost." These words, when used properly, also put your response into the form of a what? A story. Remember from above, *"Facts tell, and stories sell."* Your work is not entirely done at this point but, more times than not, they will feel satisfied with this response.

The Close

Step Six then is a natural flow from Five. Now it's time to ask for the order or 'The Close.' This is not necessarily a long step. After successfully addressing the objections, all indications should be they are ready to engage. I will offer, however, that there are a number of things that need to be in place in order to be able to ask for the order. At this point, you should have created trust, demonstrated need, usability, affordability, and clarity around the product or service. The salesperson must have the chops to actually ask for the order. There has to be a level of persistence, usually used to work through objections but also needed when the sales cycle is longer than doing just one presentation. Conversely, there are a few things that need to be avoided in order to close a sale. No arguing, no knocking the competition, and no overselling allowed. Remember, this is just a conversation. Our goal is to lead them to our water and allow them to take a drink. If we pull on the rope, they are going to resist. This has to be a willing engagement and that happens when you have gained trust and demonstrated you are the gap filler.

Before we get to Step Seven, I want to throw in some important ideas regarding word choice. When we are learning needs and challenges, that's what you should be calling them – *needs and challenges*. Never use the word 'problem'. 'Problem' has a more negative connotation and may cause a negative reaction from your prospect. Also, when referring to these challenges, don't use the word 'same.' As in, "I have another client with the same challenge." Maybe it is the same, but more likely, it's similar. Something is a little different, but it isn't the same. Instead, refer to another client's challenge as 'similar.'

Ask for Referrals

Step Seven of our process is to ask for referrals. Many do not do this. I am not sure if it is fear or an expectation that they get leads from the marketing department or whatever the many reasons may be for avoiding this step. Prospecting is hard work, especially if you are new and still making cold calls. Warm leads and word-of-mouth will likely always be the best way to get new business. Do not leave satisfied customers as an untapped source of new opportunities. Periodically, ask them for a referral.

Bonus Material

First, I promised a peek at how to make your communication better with a prospect or client. The way to do that is by using a DiSC assessment. No, you are not going to ask your prospect to take an assessment. Hopefully, your organization likes to use assessments to help everyone in the office communicate more effectively. Within each DiSC communication/behavioral style, there are tells that you can use to be more appealing to your prospect. There is a phrase used a lot now called "Meeting someone where they are." You can use a DiSC assessment to do just that. You are meeting the prospect where they are from a behavioral style perspective. Send me an email and I will send you some free information on how to learn and leverage this concept: jdiebold@focalpointcoaching.com.

The other item I would like to address is time management. This is a huge deal for salespeople. Many are working virtually now, but many are also back to in-person meetings. This means windshield time. Time is our most precious resource and for a salesperson, that couldn't be truer. Here is a simple question I want to offer to sales leaders: what activities should your salespeople be engaged in the vast majority of the time? I know. Seems like a rhetorical question. But inside many organizations, salespeople do a lot of marketing, internal meetings, parts running, and many other things that aren't actually selling. What can you do as an organization to make sure your salespeople are selling *more* than they are doing other things?

I don't have the space to provide greater detail. The information given is some of the most effective from each category. Being intentional about implementing these practices will improve your effectiveness as a salesperson or sales leader. Don't be in the 60% of organizations that admit to random or informal sales training practices. And provide training regularly so it isn't "forgotten within three months."

I became a certified FocalPoint coach and trainer to utilize my decades of experience and help organizations grow faster than they thought possible. Follow me on LinkedIn. My posts may provide some helpful insight. Also, if you are a sales leader, I encourage you to check out the Sales Leader Roundtable www.salesleaderroundtable.com. This cohort was created for sales leaders to share and learn collectively. I hope these few pages helped spur some thoughts to help you create or validate your sales process.

I look forward to learning more about your organization.

***

To contact Jim:

www.jimdiebold.focalpointcoaching.com

www.linkedin.com/in/jim-diebold

jdiebold@focalpointcoaching.com

1 - https://taskdrive.com/sales/sales-statistics/

2 - https://taskdrive.com/sales/sales-statistics/

3 - https://spotio.com/blog/sales-statistics/#salestraining

John Verrico

An internationally recognized expert in effective communication, leadership, and employee engagement, John Verrico has more than four decades of experience in senior communication and public affairs positions. His multi-faceted background includes extensive experience in the military, government, non-profit, corporate, small business, and entertainment industries.

John is former President of the National Association of Government Communicators and served in the U.S. Navy and Navy Reserve, gaining extensive experience as a public, community, and internal communication professional before retiring as a Master Chief Journalist and continuing to hone his skills in federal and state government agencies.

An under-sized youth often victimized by bullies, John gained hope and strength from classic monster movies where he learned that even the little guy could win with a little confidence, self-awareness, communication, and a well-lit torch.

He combined all of this background, including experiences gained in multiple other occupations earlier in his career, and founded Share Your Fire, LLC, to aid aspiring and established leaders fire up their own torches – illuminating organizational climate, culture and relationships – and create healthier and more productive work environments and motivated teams.

John earned a master's degree in organizational leadership from Norwich University and a Bachelor's in Communication from the University of the State of New York.

The Enrichment of Change
by John Verrico

"Life is about growing, learning, and becoming. You cannot grow, learn, or become if you cannot embrace the changes in your life."
~Steve Rizzo

If you were asked if you would want everything in your life to remain *exactly* as it is right now, in this very moment – your health, finances, work situation, house, car, everything -- what would you say?

More likely than not, you'd admit you would want *something* to change.

Maybe you'd hope someone in your life were healthier or the pain in your knee would go away. Maybe you'd want to change some work processes. Maybe you wish it would rain or stop raining (depending on the current weather). Maybe you're vying for a different job, want a new car, are planning to redecorate something at home, or are looking to move. Maybe you wish your teenager would clean up his room. Perhaps you want to clear up your debt or get your college loan paid off. Maybe there is something you wish would change in a personal relationship. Perhaps you want to have more money. (By the way, if you want less money, please contact me and I will do my best to assist you.)

Whatever it is, there is likely always something that we wish would change.

Yet, if you were asked if you wanted to **be changed** or that you couldn't choose what changed and how, what would your reaction be?

Surely, 99% would resist.

Change happens to all of us. Some changes we want, some not.

And when faced with change, it can get a little frightening.

Changes We Seek

If you are buying a new car or moving into a new house or taking a new job or having a child – there can be so much angst and second-guessing about those decisions.

Can we afford the new expenses? Will I be able to succeed in this new position? Am I fit to be a parent? Am I ready to take on the responsibility for another person for the rest of my life?

And every change likely causes other changes. Some anticipated and some that maybe we didn't consider at first.

For example, several years after our older cat, Oliver, took his trip over the rainbow bridge, and during the lapse in social interaction during the COVID-19 pandemic, my wife and I decided to adopt a kitten that was wandering around in our neighborhood. She was cute and cuddly and full of love and playfulness that brought us joy.

She also brought lots of additional changes. There were unbudgeted veterinary expenses, we lost a portion of our pantry to cans of cat food, we had to clean a litter box a couple times a day, she was curious and getting into everything, she thought bedtime was playtime and she pounced on us and wrestled our feet when we were trying to go to sleep.

And although we weren't traveling much during that time, another consideration evolved of what to do with the little fur-baby when we go away for the weekend, or a work trip, or finally go on vacation.

So, we kept asking ourselves, did we make the right decision? Then we considered getting another kitten so that she had a playmate who could absorb some of that crazy kitten energy (we ultimately did). Before making decisions like this – or any decision – we usually evaluate our options. We weigh the pros and cons, the plusses and minuses, and decide how much change we are willing to make to achieve a desired outcome.

Note: the key part of that statement was "how much change we are *willing* to make."

Some people may call these changes sacrifices because we are changing things we are comfortable with.

A perfect example is marriage.

Marriage is probably the biggest change decision of our life. And it requires that we make a lot of behavioral changes.

For me, it was a major big deal and a decision full of fear.

Our fears are based on our own past experiences and perceptions. I had been burned in some prior relationships and, for a while, had built up some emotional defenses, ultimately joining the Navy and not allowing myself to get close to anyone.

I was fearful of trusting anyone so deeply, especially when I wasn't going to be physically around for as much as eight months at a time while at sea in some distant part of the world. Plus, I had seen so many military marriages and relationships flounder because of the physical separations. So, in my mind, there was no way I was going to get seriously involved with anyone at that point in my life.

But then I met a woman who changed my whole outlook on the world.

I was terrified of her. I was terrified of the changes I was going to make in my lifestyle in order to be with her – "sacrificing" my freedom, opening myself up to the potential for another broken heart.

But I was even more terrified of losing her and missing out on the opportunity to enrich my life with her in it.

And, of course, she was going through the same mental and emotional anxieties herself. After all, she was contemplating marrying a sailor, of all things!

Still, it came down to looking at our options, evaluating how much *we were willing to change* in order to be with each other, and then deciding upon the action to take.

The choice became obvious and, fortunately, all our fears were unfounded. The changes in our lives turned out to certainly be worth the risks. For me, marrying Bonnie was the best decision of my life. I think she feels the same (at least she says she does).

Sometimes, when facing great change, we may overthink and get stuck in a cycle of indecision and miss what could be fantastic opportunities.

Imagine if I had waffled so much, locked up in fear and indecision, that Bonnie ultimately lost interest and I lost her to someone else.

So often people are overcome by decidophobia and get deadlocked into indecision because they fear the changes that will come.

Sometimes, from the outside, a choice may seem simple. Two completely different outcomes, perhaps, and you either prefer one outcome or the other. Spending the rest of your life with the partner you love or keeping the freedom of being single.

A lot to consider, but extremely different outcomes to compare.

Choices are harder when the options are closely similar, and you need to choose between two things that are very much like each other.

For example, choosing whether or not to adopt a kitten was much easier when there was only one kitten available, but trying to choose one from amongst a litter of cuteness can be downright traumatic.

And, of course, things aren't always as simple as choosing a kitten or deciding whether or not to propose marriage.

Quite often, we are faced with change where neither option is a great one, so we are stuck with choosing between two, or several, lesser outcomes.

We may not always be happy with the choices we have, and in being fearful of being stuck with something we may regret later, we may opt not to decide and let whatever happens happen.

And if we don't voice our concerns or trepidations, and the decision is left to someone else who may not be aware of the potential impacts, we wind up dealing with change that was made by others.

And that's where things really get even more complex and challenging.

Changes that Happen to Us

Up to this point we've talked about changes where we have a say in the outcome, but we all know that is not always the case.

Quite often, we don't have options about what or how something changes and when, and we have to adapt to whatever the new norm becomes. Sometimes, change may be unexpected or even unwelcome.

We expect things in our life to go a certain way.

We plan our day, our week, and our life based upon those expectations.

Invariably, something changes.

Anytime anything changes, those expectations are shattered. We don't know what we're going to face – and even if it is better than what our "normal" is – that unknowing is what we fear.

When change happens to us, it can cause very significant biological, physical and emotional responses.

Change can be extraordinarily fearful. The thing about change is that it means moving away from something that is familiar, something that we know or have a certain level of comfort with and moving to something new and unfamiliar.

There is a certain comfort level with familiarity, and that comfort comes simply from knowing what to expect.

Going from the familiar to the unknown is, at best, intimidating, if not outright terrifying. People tend to prefer dealing with a known entity – even if it may be a terrible situation – rather than the insecurity of not knowing what's ahead.

This fear is the basis of why people stay with degrading bosses, abusive spouses, unrewarding jobs, poor housing or other disagreeable situations. How many times have we heard the expression, "better the devil you know than the devil you don't?"

I am sure we have all gone through changes that were beyond our control, that we had no input to, nor any influence on.

Sometimes they worked out. A break-up led to meeting the love of our life. After losing our job, we got a great new position. What seemed like a stupid idea at work, wound up making things easier or even enjoyable.

Other times the outcome was not so pleasant.

Having worked in the military and government agencies for more than four decades, I experienced dramatic changes every couple of years when we would get a new boss.

What happens when a new boss comes in? Sometimes we luck out and the new boss is great or an improvement on the previous one. New policies or procedures are perhaps simple to implement and make things easier or better.

Sometimes this isn't the case, and the new boss comes in like a logger, swinging the axe to cut programs, budget and sometimes even positions. Or make sweeping changes without taking the time to even get to know the organization, its mission, or its people.

One of the most demoralizing statements I've heard, and unfortunately heard it often, was, "I have been appointed here to FIX this organization." As if we were a bunch of misbehaving children. Why is the assumption always that things are broken and new bosses seem to feel they need to redo everything?

You'll notice I used the term "boss" and not "leader" and that's because sometimes we are stuck with a new person in charge that does not exhibit leadership skills. But that is a separate discussion for a whole different type of book.

Nevertheless, despite the potential for change to lead to something good in the long run, when initially faced with a pending change that we have no control over, the assumption usually seems to be that things are going to be worse than they are now, or that the change process will be painful.

The Fear of Change

As a society, we seem to be reluctant to change. The nation's epidemic of obesity and other persistent health problems are not because of some obscure "crisis in the quality or availability of healthcare but is because people have a hard time making changes in their behaviors.

According to a report in the Global Medical Forum, "Most people are sick because of how they choose to live their lives, not because of environmental factors or genetics."

More than 83 percent of the nation's total multibillion dollar healthcare budget are caused by five recurring behavioral issues. I am sure you can guess what they are.

Yep. Smoking, overeating, excessive drinking, not enough exercise, and stress.

Note, these are the same exact behavioral factors that have been responsible for most health issues since the 1950s. We all know these things are bad for us, but it is oh, so difficult to change behaviors we have become comfortable with.

We are hardwired to resist change. It goes back to our reptilian roots. As reptiles grow and change, they shed their outer skin.

If you've ever gotten a major sunburn to the point where the dead skin starts peeling off in sheets, you know that itch and discomfort. You can only imagine what it might feel like when your entire body peels at the same time.

When reptiles molt, the first thing to happen as their skin prepares to shed is a protective film forms over their eyes which effectively makes them blind throughout the change process. They can't see what's around them and what is happening, so they feel threatened. Everything around them becomes a threat. Anyone who has ever had snakes or lizards for pets will tell you to leave them alone and stay away from them during a molt.

With this in mind, we begin to understand our baseline fear of change.

Our self-talk, our thinking, can be our worst enemy in all of this. Our world is how we think of it. If we think it is bad, it is. If we think it is good, it is.

Psychologists have shown that, in general, people have several anchoring beliefs about change:

- Change means I will face new situations that will make me uncomfortable, anxious, or inadequate.
- By changing, I will be allowing myself to be exploited.
- The unknown is dangerous and uncertain.
- Change requires effort and will be painful.

You can see why they are called 'anchoring beliefs' – because they *anchor* us in place and keep us from moving forward.

But remember, we have choices in everything. We can't always choose the changes that we are forced to deal with, but we can control how we react to those changes.

The Truths about Change

There are five key truths to consider when facing change:

1. Change is the one constant you can count on. Everything changes, so if we expect change to happen, it is easier to face when it does.
2. It's usually not personal. You're not the only one dealing with change or going through this kind of challenge.
3. Change isn't the enemy, fear is. If we stop fearing change, we can address ourselves to dealing with it, accepting it, possibly even embracing it, or leading it.
4. There's a predictable emotional cycle to change. Understanding that all the emotions we are feeling are natural and should be expected, helps you to recognize those feelings for what they are. Interestingly, the same part of our brain that deals with our reaction to change is the same that deals with our comfort zone.

   Because change may represent an end to what we are familiar with – it becomes symbolic with the death of our comfort zone. So the cycle of emotions we experience when dealing with unwanted or unexpected change are similar to the grief cycle: denial, anger, bargaining, depression, and, finally, acceptance
5. You are more resilient than you think you are. You must believe in yourself. No matter what, you can get through even the toughest change.

In the end, no matter what happens to you, you are still you. As Maya Angelou said, "You may not control all the events that happen to you, but you can decide not to be reduced by them."

One additional thing to keep in mind is that this is a continuing cycle. Going back to the first truth, remember that everything changes – and each time we experience change, it makes us more prepared for the next.

Change happens. We go through our grief process until we accept it. Once we accept change, our options expand – we know what we can or cannot do. Then we can take action to function or even thrive in the new situation, and by taking that action, we strengthen our adaptability. And being adaptable, we are ready to face the next change.

We cannot experience the full richness of life stagnating in our comfort zones. Each change we face – even difficult or challenging ones – tests our limits, expands our options, and provides us an opportunity to grow, learn and become enriched by the experience.

The choice is ours.

***

To contact John:

John Verrico – Share Your Fire

https://www.johnverrico.com
https://www.linkedin.com/in/johnverrico/
https://www.facebook.com/johnverricospeaks\
https://twitter.com/jverrico
https://www.instagram.com/johnverrico/
https://soundcloud.com/johnverrico

Helen Kagan

A scientist, psychologist, artist, pioneer in creating art with intention to heal, creator of her unique concept HealingArts™ of 30 years, Dr. Helen Kagan synergistically integrates Fine Art & Art of Healing, is shown in multiple International online & physical venues, galleries, media including Artsy.net, Fox40 News, Star Tribune, ArtExpo NYC, Spectrum ArtBasel, various podcasts. Helen was awarded by PassionVista International as Woman-Leader 2023.

Dr. Kagan is a member of Artrepreneur, VoyageMia, FineArtAmerica, ISFP, VT ArtGuide, and other Platforms. As Internationally recognized author Dr. Kagan is an executive contributor to Brainz and PassionVista Magazines with her own columns, published in Authority, ThriveGlobal, Published!, Insights. She co-authored the Bestseller *We're All In This Together* (2021); collaborated with Jack Canfield and other professionals in Bestseller *The Keys to Authenticity* (2023), and is working on her own two books.

In her own words:

I believe in the inter-connectedness of mind-body-spirit and art as a catalyst for healing individuals, society, and environment. I feel it's my duty to create art for healing in our turbulent times, amid World-wide crises, pandemics, wars, anxiety, stress, uncertainty. My HealingArts™ is a high vibrational sacred space for serenity & rejuvenation to encourage wellbeing, harmony, peace, and to bring healing to everyone in need.

As a severe PTSD survivor dedicated my life to helping others, my Vision and Mission is developing a unique venue integrating art, healing, fashion & design - WearableHealingArts®

to make healing through art accessible to everyone and especially deliver my HealingArts to Healthcare and Hospitality markets to enhance wellbeing.

Authenticity. Comfort Zone. Integrity. Success. Our "new normal"?

By Helen Kagan

"Success is not final; failure is not fatal. It is the courage to continue that counts."– Winston Churchill

Do you like to explore things? I do. Explore first, and then... create something that nobody's done before. There's magic in that "space of unknown" where you travel to in your dreams, something so attractive and mesmerizing it occupies your brain completely – what am I saying! – it occupies your whole being so you can't sleep until you find that solution, invent that new concept, algorithm or device, create that amazing piece of art, music, poem... I am describing an authentic creative process here. And I am sure, AI can probably describe it much better, with more sophistication, but... I am describing it from my heart. Heart that ChatGPT doesn't have. With all the world' knowledge and wisdom, AI doesn't have a Heart and a Soul, sorry. But then, is it authentic? A big question. Definitely for me who lives to indulge in creative processes - with art, music, inventions, concepts, even words! Words are not just words (especially in a foreign language) – words have power. We use them without paying attention to their true meaning. We assume people have the same understanding or share the same values and beliefs, to only find out that others usually put a different, often opposite meaning to what you thought was the only definition. Then, this problem, challenge, conflict needs to be resolved to move forward (outside of your comfort zone), find a middle ground for, be it a personal or professional relationships.

I like to find/create a mutual understanding, a (golden) middle, to reduce conflictability, find peaceful resolutions, maintain balance. Balance is very important to me as a spiritual and energy healer living and practicing Spirituality and Healing even when it was not so popular. *Exploring & creating* are probably the most rewarding experiences on my journey, when I can develop my new discovery/invention into a successful venue, bringing progress to that area. Can't say I've always been successful in my many endeavors. More often than I'd like to, my "dream projects" end up nowhere (accompanied by lots of tears, disappointment, sadness & hopelessness) and I ask myself – really? Again? What now? I can't fail again! And after every crash, I reassure myself that I do have enough strength, power, knowledge, expertise, and whatever the hell it takes, to "raise out of ashes" again, connect with my Higher Self, and start again. Begin with **Gratitude**. Start anew. Take this as another "Lesson" to learn from and continue on my journey. Can I still do that? Can I stretch my already "overstretched" comfort zone? What about You?

I am hardly familiar with how a "comfort zone" feels. I've been living outside of it. Considering my upbringing in a crazy totalitarian country, earning my multiple graduate degrees (mainly for survival), having serious traumas forming a severe PTSD I've been living with, immigrating to US as a refugee while losing everything – motherland, the right to ever come back, identity, status, money, belongings, loved ones, *language* - the very things necessary to survive in a new country… Adjusting, acculturating and assimilating, going through the new realities, learning a new language to not only be able to communicate, but to "deliver the message" – MY message, my discoveries, my creations, trying to survive, create new exciting Programs and Projects hoping that "it will be it!", but failing again, and again… And it doesn't feel less painful every next time, even though you become more skilled in dealing with "failure" - you rename it into a "learning experience" and keep going. You don't stop. Just keep going, creating new projects, inventing things, going way outside of your comfort zone. No matter how difficult it is or how impossible it seems. Practice Gratitude – find what you're thankful for. Gain new knowledge, take different Masterclasses, find new partners, hopefully find money and new resources to continue, and… voila. You are back on track - creating, learning, progressing, and evolving. Hopefully succeeding in the process, too! These are my quintessential principles I live by. This is my authentic Truth. What's yours? Don't forget somewhere in this Process to learn "letting go" otherwise it can become too overwhelming… but that's a different story for a different book :)

"You never change your life until you step out of your comfort zone; change begins at the end of your comfort zone." – Roy T. Bennett

Comfort Zone. It's so comfortable to be in, right? And we're so used to living in it that taking yourselves, even for a little bit, outside of it, can create a big problem or uncomfortability that can pull us back into our favorite comfort zone. But then, we don't grow. Simple as that – we just don't grow, we don't evolve, we don't progress thus we can't achieve success while sitting comfortably in our "comfort zone". We can forget about "overnight success" because it is usually built for years! I believe success of our "dream projects" (whatever they are), and our Mission - Vision - Purpose, directly depend on how much we can go outside of our comfort zone. But can we remain authentic when we step out of it? In my opinion, both Success and Progress are ONLY possible when we drag ourselves outside of our "comfort zone" yet remain authentic. Then, what is it - "authentic"?

Authenticity is a crucial part of being human. It involves being true to yourself and aligning your thoughts, feelings, and actions with innermost desires and values. By embracing authenticity, we can connect with your True Self and spiritual guides, connect on a deeper level with other "spiritual beings on a human Journey", release our negative energy blockages, promote greater emotional and physical well-being. While authenticity may seem like a simple concept, it can be challenging to practice consistently (i.e. 24/7!) Society often encourages conformity and "fitting in" to predefined molds/roles. However, true healing, growth and evolvement require breaking free from these constraints (i.e. stepping outside of your comfort zone!) and embracing your authentic True Self.

> *"Authenticity is the highest form of spirituality, for it requires that we be true to ourselves and the universe." - Deepak Chopra*

We all know Life can be quite chaotic, hectic, confusing, and overwhelming... Over the last few years, for sure. Were you questioning your life? Family? Your work, business, partners, whatever constitutes your Life for you. What's happening and why? How to live it now, in our "new normal" with *Dignity & Integrity*? Is it still possible? Living in fear and uncertainty, with stress coming at us on every level and dimension of our being - we end up burned out, unable to sleep, not functioning well, we find ourselves angry, dissatisfied, frustrated, unfulfilled, and just completely tired, drained, and unmotivated...

Can we still "raise out of ashes"? Regardless of the circumstances? Who is that person – an "Authentic You"? Can you still go far out of your comfort zone to challenge your new horizons? How can you live your life authentically with integrity if the whole World going insane? Can you have empathy to others if you are not well, or falling apart, or lost your business or loved ones? Can you be authentic? Authenticity – is it a constant or a variable? Decide for yourself...

Do we go in-and-out of our "authenticity zone"?

In a powerful Bestseller *The Keys to Authenticity* I have co-authored with Jack Canfield and other experts (published July 2023), one of the concepts I was exploring was: can a person be completely authentic 24/7? Or do we create a special "authenticity zone" to go every time we connect with our True Self? Is our "authenticity zone" similar to a "comfort zone"? Can we consider being authentic if we "stretch" our comfort zone, or go completely out of it? Do we continue being authentic when we live outside of our comfort zone (which I've done most of my life)? Can we still create, find ourselves in the creative "Zone" when we're outside of our "comfort zone", and all our internal and external resources are geared towards the basic survival needs? When we find ourselves in a state of complete "overwhelm" and can barely function - are we still being authentic to our True Selves, or are we just hoping that one day things will change for the better and we will somehow get out of this terrifying state of pure survival where we can't do much of anything but trying to survive... I know from my personal experience that it's often like running in a hamster wheel while exhausting and draining your resources without having any hope for a successful resolution to your many problems and growing challenges... I don't mean to paint a dark picture of how we often put ourselves in a predicament while confusing high productivity with overwhelm, success with progress, comfort zone with authenticity. Do you know how skillfully we can do that? But I do believe we can change it by **making different choices**! (read my Exec. Contributor Columns in *Brainz* and *PassionVista* Magazines). I believe that we CAN and must choose differently from those choices we've been habitually making, expecting different results. I'm bringing awareness to creating a synergistic "marriage" of authenticity, integrity, comfort zone, creativity zone, success and progress. I believe we can do this without living in an "overwhelm" state most of the time and instead - become worry-free, healthy, happy, successful, and abundant.

Can we simultaneously *step out of our comfort zone* for growth and evolvement, and *embrace authenticity*? These concepts share common ground of personal growth and emotional discomfort, but they differ in their focus, nature of exploration, and outcomes. Stepping beyond the comfort zone involves pushing external boundaries for growth, while authenticity centers on internal alignment and genuine self-expression. Balancing both can lead to a more fulfilling life where you grow, make different choices, evolve, and stay true to yourself.

Similarities of comfort zone and authenticity:

* *S*tepping out of the comfort zone and embracing authenticity often leads to *personal growth*. When you challenge your comfort zone, you confront new experiences that expand your skills and perspectives. Similarly, authenticity involves self-awareness and self-discovery, which lead to a deeper understanding of yourself and personal development.

* Both concepts involve navigating *emotional discomfort*. Stepping beyond the comfort zone can trigger anxiety or fear due to the unfamiliarity of the situation. Authenticity may require confronting vulnerabilities and expressing your true self, which can also evoke emotional unease.

Differences:

* *Nature of Exploration. Comfort Zone* refers to the boundaries of familiarity where you feel safe and at ease. Pushing beyond the comfort zone involves venturing into the unknown or taking risks. *Authenticity* involves embracing your true self, acknowledging your feelings, thoughts, and values without conforming to external expectations. It is more about inner alignment than venturing into unfamiliar territory.

* *External vs. Internal Focus. Comfort Zone* is more about external challenges and situations requiring adaptation. The focus is on overcoming external obstacles. *Authenticity* is an internal journey that involves self-reflection and introspection. It's about understanding your internal landscape and staying true to it regardless of external pressures.

* *Growth vs. Self-Expression.* Pushing beyond the *Comfort Zone* may result in tangible achievements, new experiences, and developing new skills. The emphasis is on personal growth and expanding your capabilities. In *Authenticity* - focus is on self-expression and being true to who you are. It doesn't necessarily require you to acquire new skills, but rather to embrace and express what's already within you, self-acceptance, and meaningful connections with others.

Integrity. Ability to shift.

Another essential quality – **integrity**, known to be necessary for progress and success, is about living in accordance with your values, beliefs, morals, and principles, even when it seems hard or impossible. I consider *integrity* is not something we try to achieve; it's rather what we consciously choose. It is about our everyday CHOICE. So… choose wisely! When we live with integrity, we become reliable and people trust our word; we have a good reputation, we become better and happier - in our relationships with others and ourselves. We become trustworthy. People trust us, trust in what we do, say, and offer, people have trust in us. This is paramount. How can we see clearly if we live our life with integrity?

Here's a simple 5-step formula (A.D.A.S.A.) I created to help identify your *Integrity vault*:

1. **A**uthenticate your True Self: find - value - learn from - trust it.

2. **D**efine values & beliefs. It's easier to stand for *what's right* if you know what you stand for.

3. **A**ct with the right intention. How do we know what's right? - see 2). Make conscious choices for your career, relationships, and life in general.

4. **S**trive to be honest with yourself & others - a conscious decision we make daily.

5. **A**ssert your needs and opinions. Stand up for yourself & others especially when you believe it's right. What's right? – see 2).

While examining my own values, beliefs, and my *Integrity vault* I realized that I want to add a rather non-linear variable to the above formula – an *ability to shift (*change your perspective). I feel that NOW is a critical time for many of us to be able to **shift**. To shift from fear – to love, from surviving – to thriving, despair – to happiness, illness – to wellness, from war - to peace. For instance, my HealingArts™ - is the creative foundation for my own *shift* to Love, Gratitude & Abundance. What's yours?

20 years ago, I had to make another one of my many *shifts*… when I was found on a street in New York and delivered to ER with suspected heart attack (thanks God it was just massive panic attack due to burnout, overworking, end of marriage, tons of distress, etc. etc.). Preceding this life-altering event there were many others where I had to 'sharpen my survival skills' - which to me felt totally authentic. Those experiences included growing up in the former USSR - a totalitarian, regime-run country, antisemitism, my own clinical death, sexual abuse, immigration, being a refugee, multiple losses, and other life-shattering scenarios. However, they made me not only learn survival, but more importantly, live beyond those events (go way out of my "comfort zone") in my own authentic paradigm, while living with dignity, integrity, and in gratitude. I believe it all comes down to being authentic with your True Self. Still, I lost it many times…

Success. Failure. Progress.

My HealingArts™ was born 30 years ago when I first practiced healing as a holistic practitioner in NYC. Being a scientist, psychologist & therapist helped me to conceptualize and develop my unique approach, being a healer and artist - to express it in soulful ways to touch your Heart and uplift your Spirit. I was devoted to creating culturally-competent clinics for disenfranchised immigrant populations – from scratch, with my 'broken English,' and zero resources available. I worked 3 jobs - successfully developed and ran clinical Programs, hosted international delegations coming to learn, featured in The NY Times and on TV, developed my healing practice using multiple energy-healing modalities. I was helping people heal in many different and creative ways, called myself a 'holistic psychotherapist' (sounded quite provocative *then*), my HealingArts blossomed serving people in need, and I was happy doing authentically what I loved. Then I burned out. Completely. That's when I was picked up by Ambulance from the streets in Manhattan. Soon after that ER episode, my multiple traumas got re-activated from the amount of stress trying to not only survive, but live my Purpose, Vision, and Mission. My complex-PTSD came to bloom without asking my permission. I had to stop working all together, which was devastating. I was totally crushed. I didn't know how to be sick – that was a new "lesson" I had to learn. It was NOT authentic as I only learned how to survive. But I knew I had to bring myself back. I had to get back to normal – my "new normal", whatever it meant.

My HealingArts™ became an authentic source for my own healing which I've been bringing to the world since, offering my unique way of ***healing through art***. I believe art heals, I live through art – it is my spiritual path, transformational process, a way of being. Synergistically integrating fine art, expressive arts, and the art of healing, my colorful HealingArts™ enhance well-being, bring love and gratitude to feel authentic, joyful, and alive.

I made lots of interesting discoveries and inventions while looking for my "new self. I invented and tried to patent HQ – Holistic Intelligence™. As a holistic therapist I was excited about its authentic use in many fields. Nowadays my HQ is mainly replaced by AI which is taking us by storm! It is undoubtedly evolutional but very sad & challenging to some, especially to us, creatives.

Then, I invented ArtSynergism™ - for artists to synergistically collaborate following magical "creative Flow" being in a "Zone" (like musicians' Jam-sessions). I worked together with several artists, but the most rewarding experience was with Garsot, a well-known Greek artist (now deceased) with whom we created true masterpieces. But… we didn't succeed either.

Then, I invented Healing Zone™ & 5D Healing Room™, tried to patent them for meditation and game industries. But… had to take a pause due to lack of resources. Am waiting for the right partners/investors to come along.

Then, in the midst of Covid pandemics, when everything suddenly seemed impossible and falling apart, when all Galleries got closed, shows cancelled (I had 3 Solo Shows of 100 pieces each scheduled in major international locations - all cancelled and I was crashed again), I invented and trademarked my Wearable HealingArts®. It took a lot of effort, time (working 25/8), creativity, resources, Heart & Soul... It is finally live, beautiful, promising, and just waiting for the right people to come along - www.WearableHealingArts.com.

You think all my innovative creative projects and concepts, venues, art and healing endeavors became a success? Nope. I am sure many of you can relate. It also depends on how you define success. My inventions – they all constitute progress. Some of them are evolutional. They're my "babies" and I love them all dearly. For a creative – it is critical to keep creating, stay inspired, even when a result is not what you planned and hard worked for... I still believe we must keep creating regardless of the outcome, we need to go beyond our comfort zone while being authentic, keeping our Vision & Mission to live on Purpose.

I was so happy when years ago I came up with an idea of Wearable HealingArts™ **and last year was able to bring it to life! It was a dream come true** - a vehicle for my unique art to be "transported" to people who can't afford an original painting but can easily purchase beautiful designer garments or colorful household items from my HealingArts™ boutique Collections with high-vibrational healing energies so needed in our turbulent times. It feels *authentic* to continue creating my unique art with healing intention, while more people all over the world can benefit from having my colorful healing creations in their environment.

Our "new normal"?

I don't believe in "mistakes". I believe there're "Lessons" given for us to learn, and if we have not learned the first time, they will be given again, and again – to finally realize what we need to do to succeed. We need to define our WHY-s. I think I am finally clear about mine. I chose to be an Artist I was born to be, which allows me to live authentically because it's my Truth. But it took me almost 40 years to realize that I must do it because it is WHO I AM!

My Big Dream, Vision and Mission is to deliver my unique HealingArts™ (artworks) and WearableHealingArts® (wearables made of my art), especially to Healthcare and Hospitality markets to promote healing and enhance wellbeing. I envision "hospital-wear" and "hotel-wear" serve as healing agents to patients, Doctors, clients, staff, visitors, to experience positive impact of my art in real time, on on-going basis, guaranteed :)

My Healingarts™ - is my unique way to help *heal* the World. It is a healing tool that can help on your journey to your wellbeing, authentic Self, Mission, Purpose, Success.

Success - is a journey requiring a multitude of strategies, including authenticity, integrity, trust, perseverance, collaboration, dedication. Being true to myself and staying committed to high ethical standards; having a strong sense of Purpose and working synergistically towards Mission and Vision; building trusting relationships and persevering through challenges; finding joy and practicing gratitude. These are my key ingredients for Success. – Helen Kagan

***

To contact Helen:

www.HelenKagan.com

www.WearableHealingArts.com

Afterword

Life and business are always a series of transitions… people, places, and things that shape who we are as individuals. Often, you never know that the next catalyst for improving your business and life is around the corner, in the next person you meet, next mentor you hire or the next book you read.

Jim Britt has spent over four decades influencing individuals and entrepreneurs with strategies to grow their business, developing the right mindset and mental toughness to thrive in today's business environment and to live a better life overall. Allowing all you have read in this book to create a new you, to reinvent yourself and your business model if required, because every business and life level requires a different you. It is your journey to craft.

Cracking the Rich Code is a series that offers much more than a book. It is a community of like-minded influencers from around the world. A global movement. Each chapter is like opening a surprise gift, that just may contain the one idea that changes everything for you. Watch for future releases and add them to your collection.

The work of Jim Britt has filled seminar rooms to maximum capacity and created a worldwide demand. If you get the opportunity to attend one of his live events, jump at the chance. You'll be glad you did.

Become a coauthor: If you are a coach, speaker, consultant of entrepreneur and would like to get the details about becoming a coauthor in the next Cracking the Rich Code book in the series, contact Jim britt at: support@jimbritt.com

STRUGGLING WITH MONEY ISSUES?

Check out Jim's latest program "Cracking the Rich Code" which focuses on the subconscious programs influencing one's financial success, that keeps most living a life of mediocrity. This powerful four-month program is designed to change one's relationship with money and reset your money programming to that of the wealthy. More details at: www.CrackingTheRichCode.com

To Schedule Jim Britt as a featured speaker at your next convention or special event, online or live, email: support@jimbritt.com

Master each moment as they become hours that become days.

Make it a great life!

Your legacy awaits.

STAY IN TOUCH

www.JimBritt.com

www.JimBrittCoaching.com

www.CrackingTheRichCode.com

www.PowerOfLettingGo.com

www.JimBrittAcademy.com

www.ingramcontent.com/pod-product-compliance
Lightning Source LLC
LaVergne TN
LVHW021810060526
838201LV00058B/3319